Collecting the Dots

Problem Formulation and Solution Elements

MARTIN C. LIBICKI,
SHARI LAWRENCE PFLEEGER

OP-103-RC

January 2004

RAND SCIENCE AND TECHNOLOGY

This research in the public interest was supported by RAND, using discretionary funds made possible by the generosity of RAND's donors, the fees earned on client-funded research, and independent research and development (IR&D) funds provided by the Department of Defense.

ISBN: 0-8330-3561-4

The RAND Corporation is a nonprofit research organization providing objective analysis and effective solutions that address the challenges facing the public and private sectors around the world. RAND's publications do not necessarily reflect the opinions of its research clients and sponsors.

RAND® is a registered trademark.

Published 2004 by the RAND Corporation
1700 Main Street, P.O. Box 2138, Santa Monica, CA 90407-2138
1200 South Hayes Street, Arlington, VA 22202-5050
201 North Craig Street, Suite 202, Pittsburgh, PA 15213-1516
RAND URL: http://www.rand.org/
To order RAND documents or to obtain additional information, contact
Distribution Services: Telephone: (310) 451-7002;
Fax: (310) 451-6915; Email: order@rand.org

Preface

Across a wide variety of endeavors—from homeland security to foreign intelligence, criminal investigation, public health, and system safety—failure to anticipate disaster has been ascribed to the inability to "connect the dots." This paper argues that to "connect the dots," one must first "collect the dots." All too often, the inability to foresee trouble has come about because pieces of information sit in this or that head. Were they combined, trouble would be easier to foresee, but when each stands alone, no compelling conclusions suggest themselves. This paper investigates some of the barriers to circulating telltale information and describes some approaches—institutional, social, and technological—that would begin to bring information together in a meaningful way.

This paper results from the RAND Corporation's continuing program of self-sponsored independent research. Support for such research is provided, in part, by donors and by the independent research and development provisions of RAND's contracts for the operation of its U.S. Department of Defense federally funded research and development centers. It is expected to be of interest to the broad policymaking community, particularly those who are concerned about how to recognize and thereby avert disastrous events.

RAND Science and Technology

The RAND Corporation is a nonprofit research organization providing objective analysis and effective solutions that address the challenges facing the public and private sectors around the world. RAND Science and Technology (S&T), one of RAND's research units, assists government and corporate decisionmakers in developing options to address challenges created by scientific innovation, rapid technological change, and world events. RAND S&T's research agenda is diverse. Its main areas of concentration are science and technology aspects of energy supply and use; environmental studies; transportation planning; space and aerospace issues; information infrastructure; biotechnology; and the federal R&D portfolio.

Inquiries regarding RAND Science and Technology may be directed to

Stephen Rattien
Director, RAND Science and Technology
RAND
1200 South Hayes Street
Arlington, VA 22202-5050
703-413-1100 x5219
www.rand.org/scitech

Contents

Figures

Tables

Summary

The prevailing view in the intelligence and public safety communities is that forestalling major threats such as terrorist attacks or epidemics requires weaving together disconnected pieces of information to reveal broader patterns; in more common terms, we call this "connecting the dots." In this paper, we argue that connecting the dots is less likely to happen unless one takes a prior step: "collecting the dots," that is, bringing scattered pieces of information into some proximity to each other to enable pattern recognition. This paper is intended to help decisionmakers understand the dimensions of solving the problem of "collecting the dots." Any solution involves identifying what information is important and improving its circulation within communities that are in a position to connect the dots so collected. The paper describes organizational and informational barriers to "collecting the dots" and explores the characteristics of potential solutions to overcoming them.

Assumptions and Methodology

We made three basic assumptions about the scope of the problem. First, we restricted the problem at hand to dealing with explicit information rather than with knowledge management as a whole. Second, we focused on understanding how to collect and communicate dots on new or rare phenomena the existence of which is indicated by the dots (that is, by newly collected or reconsidered information).

And third, we looked primarily at how information is identified and shared in large communities. In this context, "large" means greater than the size (variously defined as between 50 and 200 people) at which everyone in the community knows one another.

We analyzed several historical examples of well-known failures to "collect the dots" in order to identify those things that might encourage or discourage collection. Next, we reviewed a subset of the literature on information networks, knowledge management, and institutional communication, enhancing our understanding not only of what we know about aspects of our problem but also highlighting those areas where gaps in our understanding occur. We also created and ran a heuristic model that simulated the flow of information within an organization, in an attempt to understand variations in the flow of "useful" versus "misleading" information.

Barriers

There are four major barriers to circulating the right kinds of information within communities.

- *Lack of awareness.* People who possess notable information may not be aware of its notability and thus may not circulate it widely. As such, an important aspect of awareness may involve recognizing when one possesses some of the "dots" and therefore needs to circulate information to help others assemble the "bigger picture."
- *Lack of attention.* Attention is the obverse of awareness. Whereas awareness leads to information flow, attention focuses on information received. Attention needs to be highly selective; paying attention to too many "dots" decreases the likelihood that significant items will receive needed attention.
- *Inadequate templates.* Templates are generalized patterns based on experience that help people understand new situations. In some cases, past experience does not map usefully onto new information. Observers may try to squeeze new information into

templates prematurely or to fit information into inadequate, inappropriate templates, thus closing off potential avenues of interpretation.

- *Compartmentalization.* Sometimes people in subcommunities tend (for security and bureaucratic reasons) to keep information to themselves. This careful guarding keeps information from circulating, thereby preventing dot collection.

Some Solution Approaches

In one sense, the problem of collecting the dots is one of promoting information-sharing in order to accelerate the detection of critical phenomena. To some extent, solutions that promote the sharing of information correspond to the barriers cited (e.g., networking helps to mitigate compartmentalization). In other respects, just as biochemical excitation agents do not simply suppress inhibiting agents, some solutions take the barriers as given and try to overcome them in other ways.

Networking

Information-sharing requires some kind of networking. Physical networking that connects machines can be a valuable tool in bringing disparate pieces of information into proximity. Social networks that connect people are just as important, but can be more difficult to institutionalize. For one thing, communities may not be well-defined, and community boundaries may not always be clear. Individuals known as "connectors," who know and speak with many people within an organization, may have an important role to play in bolstering social networks.

Roles and Responsibilities

In any process that addresses the problems of circulating information, there are at least three types of roles: decisionmakers, perceivers, and connectors. Clarifying the responsibilities of each of them within organizations or communities can improve communications.

Collaboration

Collaboration in this case means getting the right people together in the right situation. Mechanisms may be needed to overcome a built-in reluctance to collaborate. One of the biggest challenges to promoting collaboration is getting people to share information that they alone possess.

Categorization

"Binning" similar pieces of information into consistent categories enables both machines and people to collect dots.

Hybrid Approaches

An approach that combines human and machine capabilities is promising, because it can exploit the unique capabilities of each.

Solution Frameworks

A formal process for collecting the dots should incorporate a significant role for human expertise, including heuristic tools for pattern recognition and relationships based on experience and knowledge. One possible framework would include five essential activities:

1. An in-box monitor that captures and sorts information;
2. A synthesizer that establishes contexts for messages and helps identify candidate templates for categorizing them and adding information about relationships;
3. An analyzer that picks out and juxtaposes related information, while assessing each component;
4. A decision tool that interacts with the community's decision-makers to determine and evaluate next steps; and
5. A connector that takes output from the fourth stage and transmits it to the right audiences.

Connecting the dots requires collecting the dots. Ultimately, these two activities are not separate and distinct. Further research to examine and refine the concepts introduced in this paper would look for a set of institutional and technological arrangements that would improve the likelihood of both successful collection and connection.

Acknowledgments

This essay draws, in part, on NSF and NASA proposals, which we had considerable help in writing. Tora Bikson, Craig Martell, and Katherine Carley contributed immensely to the proposals and therefore to this paper. Bill Butz, Jenny Preece, Ben Shneiderman, Felicia Wu, Charles Pfleeger, Ed Balkovich, Kevin O'Connell, and Ed O'Connell also contributed through their careful reading of earlier drafts and their insightful comments.

CHAPTER ONE
Introduction

Life is a risky pursuit, and much of what we do is aimed at understanding, mitigating, or avoiding risk. The understanding and consequent actions depend on gathering knowledge about situations and their elements, some of which are difficult to identify or describe. For example, understanding a new disease involves not only identifying the symptoms but also describing how the disease differs from other, similar illnesses. Nevertheless, we slowly build up our understanding from sometimes disparate pieces of information, some of which can change as our understanding grows. As we collect the information, we try to make sense of it in some way, so that we can interpret new or revised information in context.

Often, the information available to us has no context when it first appears. We live in a sea of "dots" of information—events, facts, relationships, and/or interpretations thereof—and it is tempting to try to "connect the dots" to help us make sense of the world around us. For example, it is widely acknowledged that success at counterterrorism (and other efforts to identify threats and avoid problems) requires that people "connect the dots"—that is, transform scattered and seemingly unrelated pieces of information into a complete picture of some situation in order to prevent an attack or respond to a threat.

In an ideal situation, the dots are sitting there, waiting to be connected—much like, say, U.S. census records, with data neatly in place and easy to find. In reality, data are seldom so neatly arranged and easily scanned; intervening steps are usually required between gathering raw intelligence and recognizing patterns that connect discrete bits of information. While the "dots" may exist—in the sense that they represent pieces of intelligence now possessed by various individuals within an organization or community of practice[1] (hereafter called a "community")—they often exist widely separated from each other, in isolated locations or isolated from one another. Indeed, they can be particularly hard to recognize. And even when a dot's existence is known, its nature or importance may be difficult to recognize or understand. For example, when someone is first learning about an issue, a person, or an incident, much of the relevant information may lie in people's heads and in various stages of articulation, difficult to divine or even describe. Those involved may recognize that something odd is nagging at them, but it is unclear whether the existence of that something is worth mentioning to someone else.

In this paper, we argue that in order to "*connect* the dots," one must first "*collect* the dots." That is, substantial data recognition, gathering, and sorting are required to facilitate the eventual connecting of dots. The key to this initial but necessary stage is bringing related but scattered facts into proximity with each other in order to help analysts detect significant patterns or connections. Admittedly, it is sometimes difficult to know which dots to collect and keep until we know their likely or actual connections to one another. That is, their connections may be what make them important, just as a link in a chain is important in supporting its adjacent links. Still, the recognition of the importance of a fact must precede its communication to others who need to know about it.

There are three ways to think about bringing facts together: combinatorial, network, and spatial. *Combinatorial proximity* exists

---

[1] An informal network of people who share similar roles working in a common context or with a similar perspective (Bieber et al., 2000). Also defined as a group of people who come together to learn from each other by sharing knowledge and experiences about the activities in which they are engaged (Wenger, 1998). The current definition, commonly used by researchers examining the dynamics of online communities, is more restrictive: professional or work-related groups that are often associated with a company or organization (Preece, 2003). We mostly use this narrower definition, because the types of problems we hope to solve generally involve organizations that are formally chartered to address them.

when there are algorithms that can recognize that two facts may be meaningfully compared to each other (e.g., they share a keyword or a tag in common). *Network proximity* exists when two facts are known by two people who tend to share information with one another. *Spatial proximity* exists when two facts exist in the same location or community, so that one member of the community might come across and recognize both of them.

Proximity can also be hybrid. For example, rules or algorithms can filter dots for presentation to an organization or community of practice (hereafter called a community), as when information is placed in a form (a table, or returns from a search query) or depicted in a graph or chart. Then, social processes or interactions make people aware of which dots merit attention. Exactly which approach or combination will work will vary by community and by problem.

In most cases, it is hoped that the ultimate result of collecting—and then connecting—the dots will be the discovery of insights, understanding, and guidance that would have been less obvious from one dot alone. The problem is thus transferred to one of pattern recognition, where the pattern is recognizable only when enough information of certain types and configurations is in place.

Pointillism is one metaphor for the way in which pieces of information are assimilated and viewed. In this style of painting, distinct specks or "points" of color are arranged to represent distinct figures and objects, recognizable only from a certain distance and perspective; the eye and the mind fill in the gaps between dots of color. Similarly, dots of information may not actually be connected, and an individual may not be able to discern meaning or pattern without adding information from other sources. It is only when the dots are *collected* and connected and thus associated with some underlying phenomenon that people can identify the proper relationships and see the canvas as it is.

Because the eye and mind play such an important role, the perspective and context of the viewer influence what conclusions are drawn. That is, any one dot may contribute to the resolution of many different pictures; it may be interpreted differently depending on where it sits, where viewers sit, and what viewers see. And a particular individual must be alert to the possibility of identifying and making sense of the dots; someone who is not looking is far less likely to see.[2]

Thus, the problem we address is how to identify and collect dots before we can consider connecting them. Our analysis is performed in four steps. First, we introduce dot collection as a phenomenon affecting large organizations and communities. We illustrate as much by exploring several examples of failures to collect the dots, in domains ranging from war and counterterrorism to crime, public health, space exploration, and even automobile manufacturing. Second, we characterize some of the obstacles to collecting the dots. Third, we contemplate systematic approaches to developing organizational capabilities to collect the dots more efficiently; we also describe an informal model of how information might circulate within organizations. The model's implications suggest several next steps toward improving circulation effectiveness. Fourth, we outline a research agenda that proposes to further characterize the problem, to provide a basis for investigating each of the problem's aspects—and possible solutions—in greater depth.

Dimensions of the Problem: Historical Failures

Dot collection examples abound, in that history provides many instances of the failure to identify and circulate important information (or at least in time to take needed action). These examples are instructive both in illustrating why dots should be collected and in suggesting barriers to doing so. Although they are predominantly from the world of public policy, the examples we present span a variety of experience, from war and crime to public health and systems perform-

---

[2] Tools can encourage this identification. They can help by filtering information, highlighting dots of a particular type, using data mining techniques to flag unusual situations, and so on.

ance. The problem we address appears widely throughout modern complex societies.[3]

We begin by nothing that there are two kinds of interactions among people or groups. The simpler kind, called *symmetric,* occurs when people have similar roles in solving a problem—and hence collecting or connecting the dots. They tend to have similar jobs, and often have corresponding worldviews, interests, or backgrounds; in a sense they speak the same language. The second kind, called *asymmetric,* involves people who have dissimilar roles in solving a problem—and hence different responsibilities for collecting or connecting the dots. They tend to view the same things from a different perspective and they often have different backgrounds or interests.

Symmetric combinations of information characterize the first four examples: the terrorism, epidemic, sniper, and Pearl Harbor cases. In symmetric cases, the community of practice is composed of people with similar duties, in possession of comparable facts. Symmetric cases present indications that are more parallel (e.g., patients presenting the same symptoms) or less parallel (e.g., the clues that would permit inference of a Japanese attack on Pearl Harbor). Here, it may be said that one fact is noise but two facts are signal. That is, a lone fact, by itself, may not be terribly indicative of anything but the normal range of human behavior or circumstance. Two facts, however, may suggest that some underlying causal factor is at play, giving rise to a set of anomalies falling outside the range of statistical variation (absent an underlying cause). Anomalies themselves do not lead

---

[3] There is a reason that most of the examples are drawn from public policy. Modern societies tend to assign to government the task of protecting against certain types of unlikely but broad catastrophic events that no one individual can cover adequately. It is in the nature of military affairs, counterterrorism, and epidemiology to be dominated by the unexpected. Conversely, the fate of most other enterprises, especially commercial ones, is less likely to depend on the inability to spot a specific disaster in the making than it is on the inability to put related important dots together on a day-to-day basis. That Enron, Tyco, WorldCom and other companies laid low in the wake of accounting scandals suggests that this distinction may be overdrawn insofar as commercial enterprises are also heir to disaster. But, in these cases, top management knew what was going on and made a concerted attempt to disguise important facts from others. These situations were largely not cases of failing to collect the dots; the dots were known but purposely kept out of sight.

to detection; there may not be enough dots to infer anything meaningful from them. But they may well induce others to start searching for similar or related examples that help paint a fuller picture; in toto, the collection may possess explanatory value.

The latter three examples—the Chinese embassy bombing, the Challenger disaster, and the airbag/security interactions—are asymmetric combinations, which characterize complex systems where changes in one facet create unexpected interactions with others. One dot is the change; the other dot is the knowledge of what a change might do. In these situations, not only are the dots dissimilar but so also are the people who know about the dots. That is, without some process for putting dots together, it is unlikely that the pieces of information would be merged to form a bigger picture. For instance, in the Chinese embassy bombing example, the officials familiar with what was where in Belgrade did not usually travel in the same circles as the person determining targets; need-to-know often prevented them from finding out meaning and implication even if they had possession of isolated information. Similarly, the NASA space shuttle manager does not always communicate with the Morton Thiokol engineers building parts for the shuttle. When automobiles are designed and constructed, the safety engineer does not always communicate enough with the security engineer. Thus, dots of information (what we know, or "knowns") can be mated to each other, or they can be mated to areas of relevance (what we need, or "needs")—often the more difficult problem. For instance, the need, "Is this target proscribed?" requires the known "Yes, it's the Chinese embassy." Similarly, one dot may be a fault or a change to a program; the other dot is the context that establishes its dire consequences.

Example One: Terrorism on September 11, 2001. In the months prior to September 11, 2001, one FBI special agent began to notice that there were many Arabs in flight school in the Phoenix, Arizona, area sporting strongly anti-American sentiments. Unbeknown to him, another agent in Minneapolis, Minnesota, was pondering why Zacarias Moussaoui had shown far more interest in piloting an aircraft than in taking off and landing it. Had these agents compared notes, they might have come closer to realizing what terrorists were planning. That is, the urgency was clearer when both pieces of information were linked than when they existed separately. In this case, the pieces of information were made visible up the hierarchy but not laterally (i.e., not to the colleagues who would have reacted with alacrity and perhaps insight if they had known the existence of both pieces of information). Similarly, the information known to the government prior to the 1998 bombings of U.S. embassies in East Africa included satellite phone records, names and aliases, terrorist-owned ships, interactions with local law enforcement (including who was released from jail after bribes were paid), and embassy surveillance by terrorists. Had the pieces been put together, the bombings might have been averted. But data were compartmentalized and the threat was not taken seriously. *Our lesson: Wide lateral circulation of unusual or distressing information may be helpful.*

Example Two: Disease identification. Many new diseases (whether natural or not) appear not with a set of clearly unique symptoms, but rather with symptoms that are similar but not identical to some existing diseases (e.g., flu-like symptoms). Doctors who observe a case of the new disease may feel that they are viewing something out of the ordinary, but they hesitate to take special action; every doctor occasionally sees something out of the ordinary that turns out to be nothing special. However, if several doctors in multiple locations were to compare notes, they might find the same odd set of symptoms showing up, suggesting the emergence of a new disease or at least a new strain of an old disease. That this is atypical is illustrated by the fact that neither AIDS, nor the Hantavirus, nor the West Nile virus was identified as such until two cases finally showed up in front of one doctor. Here, linking the facts is not enough. We also must know the credibility and context of each piece of information and have some way of assessing the credibility of the combined result. We must do this in ways that respect prevailing privacy norms (especially once correlations can be established between someone's genetics and his or her propensity to exhibit certain symptoms when struck by specific diseases). Similar examples could include links between circumstances and affliction, as with environmentally caused asbestosis or with Mad Cow disease. *Our lesson: Systematic discovery processes may be needed.*

Example Three: The Beltway sniper. In the case of the Beltway sniper, almost all law enforcement agencies in and around Washington, D.C., were focused on cracking the case and had collectively set up clearinghouses and teams to do so; there was no lack of attention at the time of the shootings (although how, when, by whom, where, and at what cost the crime would be cracked may have differed among jurisdictions). The key clue was the blue Chevrolet Caprice, which had first been reported as being slowly driven away from the killing in the District of Columbia. A similarly described car had been linked to a shooting several weeks earlier at Hillandale (in eastern Montgomery County), but only later were the sniper's spree and the Hillandale shooting (where no one actually died) associated. In this case, weak signals were overwhelmed by noise: the spurious clue of "the white man in the white van." Of course, the distinction between noise and too many dots may be obvious only in retrospect; there are millions of potential dots—some are part of one picture, some part of another, and most part of nothing. It is not easy keeping multiple conflicting patterns in play in the face of a strong desire to jump to conclusions. *Templates* are generalized patterns drawn by people from their experience to help them understand new situations (Klein, 1998). In some cases, templates are useful in putting together disparate pieces of a problem to point to a solution. In this case, the chosen template was misleading. *Our lesson: Avoid being locked into templates prematurely.*

Example Four: Pearl Harbor. This example comes from Roberta Wohlstetter's description of the bombing of Pearl Harbor (Wohlstetter, 1962). She argues that the reason that the Pearl Harbor invasion, for which there were many signals, was unforeseen was because of noise (e.g., feints, panics) that had been generated over the prior two years. Yet within her narrative we find many stories where information was known by a few but not known by enough. The Army and the Navy hierarchies in Hawaii did not communicate enough of the right information; neither did forces in the field nor staff in headquarters. Sometimes position in the military hierarchy discouraged wider circulation of unwelcome news; no one wanted to tell a higher-up about unusual behavior, and underlings often had little credibility with their superiors. Some threshold has to be exceeded before people pay attention to notable events. In the Pearl Harbor example, the noise level was sufficient to drown out the signal, in part because the noise was known to many, but also because each signal was known only to a few, and so the signal did not break through the noise level. *Our lesson: Flexible templates and lateral circulation may help extract signal from noise.*

Example Five: Embassy bombing. A NATO-dropped bomb hit the Chinese embassy in Belgrade during the Kosovo campaign (in March of 1999). It was sent to an address that, based on the maps in use, planners believed to be that of a Yugoslavian supply ministry. Strike planners were working with maps that were in fact out of date. Yet not everyone was unaware of which buildings were where in Belgrade. There were, for instance, defense attachés who had been to the new embassy (e.g., for a reception) after the Chinese moved in; many U.S. consular officials had similar knowledge. Had planners and defense attachés (or consular officers) talked, the error might have been exposed. In retrospect, the planners had a specific need; they wanted to know if there was an acceptable target at this location. In retrospect, the Defense Attachés' office (and other consular officials) had a specific piece of knowledge, namely that there was an embassy—an unacceptable target—at this location. But the planners' need and the consular officers' knowledge were not linked until it was too late. *Our lesson: Assumptions can mislead; we must first know that we need more information.*

Example Six: Car manufacturing. Many systems are so large or complex that they are designed and built by teams, wherein each team member tackles a different function or feature. This divide-and-conquer approach works well when the system's functions are completely independent of each other. But sometimes the dependencies are not clear, either because the subsystem designers do not communicate with each other or because the dependencies are hidden away. To see the effect this can have, consider the subsystems of today's typical automobile. The security subsystem makes sure the doors lock and stay locked until an authorized party tries to open them, either with a key, a remotely controlled device, or a keypad. The safety subsystem usually includes seat belts and air bags, with the latter designed to inflate when a sensor on the front or side detects a significant impact. If the two subsystems' designers do not communicate properly, the safety subsystem might be designed—as happened in one case—so that the door locks open when the airbags inflate, allowing passengers and driver to escape after a collision. But a clever thief could use this information to open a car's door by whacking the front fender very hard, causing the air bags to inflate and the locks to pop open. *Our lesson: Key behaviors may not be visible if parts are examined in isolation.*

Example Seven: Challenger explosion. The space shuttle Challenger exploded because O-rings were brittle and cracked in the sub-freezing temperatures of launch day. There were many advance warnings that the O-rings could cause problems, but the powers that be ignored them, hoping that the lack of failures in the past meant that the problem was being overstated. The decisionmakers were biased by pressure to meet a schedule, so their wishful thinking encouraged them to consider the O-ring warnings as noise instead of signal. Such thinking also enabled the disaster of the space shuttle Columbia; the ramifications of the damaged protective tiles should have been more widely communicated to those in charge of other features or subsystems. Indeed, frequently, political pressures act as noise that intrudes on those who are trying to make an objective determination of what is happening in a situation. Unfortunate examples abound, including premature announcements of success during wartime, and biased interpretation of scientific findings to support political expediency (U.S. House of Representatives 2003). *Our lesson: Signals and noise can be mistaken for one another (especially when wishful thinking intrudes).*

Methods and Scope of Inquiry

Each of the examples above offers more than just the lessons indicated. We can view the examples collectively as a body of evidence, suggesting that closer inspection can teach us not only about what went wrong but also about how to anticipate, diagnose, and prevent problems in the future. For instance, each lesson can help us determine the barriers to dot collection and connection, enabling us to put in place processes to overcome them or at least mitigate their negative effects. But such analysis requires careful use of methods to derive appropriate information in a given context. In this section, we describe the methods used to glean important facts and relationships, ultimately painting a bigger picture of the way forward in defining the dot collection problem and seeking solutions.

Our method of investigation begins by recognizing the multidisciplinary nature of the problem. That is, researchers in a wide variety of domains have studied various aspects of the problem separately, but the pieces have not been put together. We have identified relevant aspects and studied the literature in appropriately related domains of inquiry. These domains include

- Sociology, and particularly dynamic network analysis, to investigate how people communicate with each other;
- Psychology (particularly cognitive psychology), to understand how people perceive information and events, store that information in their memories, and link pieces of related information in their minds;
- Information science (particularly knowledge management), to investigate how knowledge is described, organized, and shared;
- Statistics, to investigate how to recognize anomalies and unusual situations; and
- Computer science and software engineering, to investigate how well-designed information technology can be used to improve analysis and communication.

For each discipline, we interviewed experts and read widely in the literature related to the aspect of the problem we were investigating. From the interviews and readings, we identified frameworks and approaches that offer promise in addressing the various components of the collecting-the-dots problem. As we note in later sections of this paper, these several disciplinary frameworks help to form the basis for our suggested approach to a solution.

However, it is clear that solving the most general case of collecting the dots is a formidable task. Thus, we find it important to make three basic assumptions to ensure that the problem is tractable. We discuss each in turn.

Dealing with Explicit and Tacit Knowledge

Until the 1990s, most researchers who studied knowledge generation and transfer focused primarily on *explicit* information or knowledge: facts and actions that can be described and captured (electronically or otherwise) for use by others. *Tacit* information, the knowledge portrayed in body language, intuition, and sensibility, played only a secondary role, as scientists investigated what could be represented in formal grammars and manipulated using information technology. This focus was encouraged by American business people, who placed more faith in explicit than in tacit knowledge. However, tacit knowledge was given more prominence by the work of Nonaka and Takeuchi (1995), who presented evidence that Japanese executives value tacit over explicit knowledge.

We began our investigation by examining the state of the discipline known as "knowledge management"[4] to determine what it offers us in solving our problem. Kankanhalli et al. (2003) note that there are two aspects of knowledge management that are particularly useful: codification and personalization. Codification involves developing ontologies, used to interpret and structure knowledge so that it can be stored in repositories known as knowledge bases. In a sense,

---

[4] Part of knowledge management involves learning how to develop systems under which people seek to determine who in an organization has solved similar problems before; the knowledge management systems of Siemens, Bain, and Accenture bear mention.

the ontology acts as a common language through which different people can deposit, access, and share information; it can be thought of as a mechanism for knowledge reuse. On the other hand, personalization uses direct communication to share tacit and unstructured knowledge (Hansen, Nohria, and Tierney, 1999). Techniques such as storytelling and videoconferencing, and the availability of directories of "subject matter experts," among other resources, are useful in managing this type of knowledge; such tools often address how to disseminate "know-how" (implicit or tacit knowledge) throughout a community.

Nonaka and Takeuchi (1995) point out that there is clear interaction between explicit and tacit knowledge:

- Tacit knowledge can generate new tacit knowledge during the socialization process. As people chat, they share their tacit knowledge (both purposefully and inadvertently); this is what Hansen et al. call "personalization."
- Explicit knowledge can generate new explicit knowledge, through codification and combination.
- Tacit knowledge can generate explicit knowledge through a process of externalization. As people share their tacit knowledge and understand it better, they can sometimes learn to express it more formally, thereby converting some or all of it to explicit knowledge.
- Explicit knowledge can lead to tacit knowledge through a process of internalization. As experts explain their explicit knowledge to novices, they use metaphors and analogies that become new tacit knowledge about the expertise. This transfer is similar to Rasmussen's 1986 characterization of skill-based, rule-based, and knowledge-based expertise, wherein some expertise becomes ingrained and automatic.

Figure 1.1 illustrates these transformations. We initially restrict our investigation to explicit knowledge and the ways in which this type of knowledge is shared among the members of a single community and then shared across different communities.

Figure 1.1
Generating Tacit and Explicit Knowledge

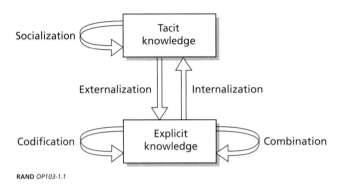

RAND *OP103-1.1*

There is substantial prior work on sharing knowledge in communities, such as McDermott, 1999a, 1999b; Wenger, McDermott, and Snyder, 2002; and Preece, 2000. Indeed, this work has established a vocabulary for distinguishing among the various ways in which knowledge may be shared. For example, Carley (2002a) defines and explains the several kinds of relationships among people, information, and needs using a meta-matrix of different kinds of networks (see Table 1.1). This work, rooted in Carnegie Mellon University's dynamic network analysis program, describes the use of social networks that allow people to communicate with each other, knowledge networks to enable people to share information, and needs networks to help people recognize each others' needs. Similarly, information networks are designed to organize information in ways that

Table 1.1
Meta-Matrix for Collecting the Dots

	People	Information	Needs
People	Social network	Knowledge network	Needs network
Information		Information network	Match network
Needs			Conditional needs network

SOURCE: Data from Kathleen M. Carley, 2002a. "Inhibiting Adaptation." In *Proceedings of the 2002 Command and Control Research and Technology Symposium,* Naval Postgraduate School, Monterey, Calif. Vienna, Va.: Evidence Based Research.

highlight similarities across differing contexts. Other networks help match needs with information or one type of need with another. Our investigation of possible solutions should include and build on the definitions and uses of metrics and models in Carley's existing framework.

Our work also takes into account the notion of volatility described by Kankanhalli et al. (2003): the rapidity of change and the need to make decisions quickly and economically. Some people and organizations must react with speed to such situations as changing market forces, impending health problems, or national security threats—these are the kinds of situations for which effective dot collection is most essential. We can characterize these situations in three ways:

- Knowledge is time-sensitive;
- Information must be current; and
- Stored information must be refreshed continuously.

As shown in Table 1.2, these situations are currently being addressed by using active methods of information retrieval, based on expert directories, direct exchange, or repositories (Clayton and Foster, 2000; Earl, 2001; Hickins, 1999; Mertins, Heisig, and Vorbeck, 2001). Codification is probably not appropriate here; it is not enough to tag information and then wait for people to find it.

Table 1.2
Types of Knowledge Management Systems

	Low-Volatility Context	High-Volatility Context
Product-based organizations	Expert directories Communities of practice	Expert directories Direct exchange Repositories
Service-based organizations	Repositories	Direct exchange

SOURCE: Adapted from Kankanhalli, Atreyi, et al. 2003. "The Role of IT in Successful Knowledge Management Initiatives." *Communications of the ACM* 46 (September): 69–73.

Our problem is different from simply acquiring knowledge and then distributing it. Areas of study related to knowledge management provide some frameworks and ideas for addressing the problem. But, as with many management disciplines, knowledge management has fuzzy borders, vague notions, and extended ambitions. To be fair, the distinction between information and knowledge is inexact. But even if we could distinguish the two, it is clear that knowledge management does not offer enough to enable a solution. Our goal is not to develop analytical techniques to systematize knowledge (e.g., to capture expertise from someone about to retire or to codify lessons learned from a completed project). Nor are we interested in the mechanics (e.g., e-mail) of how to make information broadly available within an organization. Rather, we want to know, once such mechanisms are in place, how to gather relevant information from anyone and then bring it to someone else's attention. This goal requires our casting a much wider net, to capture some understanding of attention, cognition, analysis, and more.

Examining New and Rare Phenomena

As our seven vignettes suggest, the focus of understanding how to collect and communicate dots should be on new or rare phenomena whose existence is indicated by the dots (that is, by newly collected or reconsidered information). This more difficult focus is required because phenomena that are sufficiently well understood or common can be sought already by using specific procedures. For example, there are many approaches to identifying situations that are occurring more frequently than normal, as when banks notice large or repeated withdrawals made by people or organizations for whom that pattern is not typical. Similarly, credit card companies use sophisticated techniques for flagging unusual behavior, such as large or frequent purchases made in unusual countries or for unusual products.

What we seek is significantly different. Our scope of unusual events includes not only the unexpected but also the previously unknown. For example, we can know and seek symptoms of familiar medical conditions (e.g., tuberculosis). However, we do not always see a clear path, from warnings to events, for new or rare conditions (e.g., hitherto unseen strains of tuberculosis). Similarly, business schools often teach business principles using case studies of problems encountered by corporations and the ways in which the problems were addressed. But the case study approach does not always fare well in teaching people to cope with new, unanticipated, and uncharacteristic problems. To deal with this kind of novelty, our line of investigation exploits prior and substantial research conducted in both computer security and data mining. An overview of some of this work is presented in Pfleeger and Pfleeger (2003), and details of the work can be found in Lee et al. (2001), Kantardzic (2003), Thuraisingham (2001), and Hilderman and Hamilton (2001), plus the body of knowledge associated with research in artificial intelligence that identifies unusual behaviors (Traina et al., 2000; Filho et al., 2001; Wang et al., 2002; Wu and Faloutsos, 2002; and Papadimitriou et al., 2003).

Dynamic Analysis of Large Communities

The problem we have described applies primarily to large communities. In this context, "large" means greater than the size (variously defined between 50 and 200 people) at which everyone in the community knows one another. When groups are small, informal information exchange is straightforward; to a first-order approximation, everyone talks to everyone else, and they are said to have strong ties. If some fact gnaws on someone, it is likely to be mentioned to others; supplementary or complementary facts are likely to be swiftly combined. Traditional social network analysis, and the metrics and algorithms developed therein, often do not scale well for large communities (Carley, Lee, and Krackhardt 2001). It may be more fruitful to apply dynamic network analysis and to extend existing techniques for assessing how people communicate. At the same time, we seek ways to enable people who do not ordinarily talk to each other (and are said to have weak ties) to discover one another and exchange information (either directly or through some mediated exchange). This aspect of understanding the problem leverages work such as that of Brown and Duguid (2000); Wenger, McDermott, and Snyder (2002); and Bieber et al. (2000), which investigates how communities communicate effectively, as well as work on dynamic network analysis specifically designed to deal with large-scale networks under conditions of uncertainty.

A community's shared goals can act as a lens through which communication can be analyzed. Putnam (2000) points out that as a community matures, it develops *social capital*: the shared knowledge, understanding, interests, and skills needed to achieve shared goals or solve a shared problem. Preece (2003) leverages this concept in describing communication within communities. As shown in Figure 1.2, she notes that, as people become integrated into an organization, they feel a sense of community. Their individual purposes and aspirations are superceded by an interest in attaining shared goals. Likewise, the policies that might have governed their individual behaviors are replaced by a common set of norms or standards.

The resulting social capital governs the way in which the community thinks about, tackles, and ultimately solves problems. Thus, it is important to understand how the transformation from individual-think to group-think emerges and is enriched. Preece reminds us that the transformation takes place only when accompanied by significant amounts of knowledge, empathy, and trust. The latter two qualities are especially important for solving our dot collection problem. That is, knowledge is not enough; it must be leavened with heavy doses of empathy and trust for the changes to take place. She suggests actions that may be part of the recipe for a strong community:

- Understanding people's needs;
- Clearly representing the community's purpose;
- Using minimal policies that can change as norms develop;
- Finding ways to enable knowledge creation, storage, and exchange;
- Supporting communication and socialization;
- Enabling empathy by helping people understand their similarities and common interests; and
- Encouraging trust by identifying community members and describing their past accomplishments.

Figure 1.2
The Creation of Social Capital

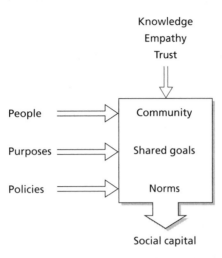

SOURCE: Adapted from Jennifer Preece, 2003. "Tacit Knowledge and Social Capital: Supporting Sociability in Online Communities of Practice." *Proceedings of I-KNOW (Third International Conference on Knowledge Management) 2003*, Graz, Austria, ed. K. Tochtermann and H. Maurer.
RAND *OP103-1.2*

Putting the Pieces Together

Simply amalgamating the findings of several disciplines will not solve the dot collection problem. Rather, any solution must come from a careful analysis of the problem from (at least) the several perspectives mentioned above, plus empirical study to enrich our understanding of communication and decisionmaking. Thus, we see the need for at least three steps:

1. *Identifying the barriers to dot collection.* In the next section, we analyze each of the seven vignettes to determine what prevented information from being recognized and communicated to the appropriate parties.

2. *Building a syncretic model.* The information that circulates within a community and across community boundaries is necessarily incomplete and varies in credibility with those who must interpret and use it. We describe a model of how information circulates within an organization or community to help us understand the factors that must be controlled in order to communicate dots effectively.

3. *Identifying the elements of a potential solution.* Using the lessons learned, existing frameworks, and model results, we suggest which elements should be part of a solution to the problem of collecting the dots.

The remainder of this paper describes these steps in detail.

Barriers to Collecting the Dots

The seven vignettes can be evaluated not only for lessons learned but also for suggested measures that might improve the ability to collect dots (as well as to enhance eventual dot connection). That is, each lesson may point to barriers to dot collection, as a strategy for searching for ways to overcome them. Four particular barriers[5] merit note: (1) lack of awareness, (2) lack of attention, (3) poor templates, and (4) compartmentalization.

Lack of Awareness

To pass a fact forward, one must be aware that it is notable. Here we mean acknowledgement of the importance of information, not just perception of its existence. There are several ways to determine whether it is something notable and not merely a result of chance. Only a small percentage of the odd is truly noteworthy; the rest sits on the tails of wide variation that characterizes human diversity.

---

[5] These are four that emerge from our analysis of the seven examples. Analysis of additional examples may suggest other barriers.

For a fact to merit consideration and be a candidate for synthesis (with other facts), it must somehow be recognized as something notable and therefore worth passing forward. There are several ways to determine whether something is notable. One is to recognize that an unusual event is not just the result of chance. Another is to narrow down an item or occurrence to a particular locale. For example, something may be hidden in one out of n haystacks of size m. To compare every pair of points to see whether they are meaningful together requires making $(n \cdot m)^2/2$ matches. If one arranges the haystacks so that two relevant points are likely to be in the same haystack, one need make only $n \cdot m^2/2$ matches—considerably fewer.

At the same time that we find something notable, we may also need to distinguish frequency-related notability from identity-related notability. That is, a frequency-related notable event is one that happens but not as often as it is happening now, or one that happens but more often than it is happening now. An identity-related event is the existence of some person or thing that matches a profile, such as when a person matches an FBI photo or fingerprint, or when a person's characteristics or actions match a published profile of characteristics or actions. There may be other ways to characterize recognition and notability. There are also different levels of notability. We can think of them as mildly different, significantly different, dramatically different, and so on. It may be that the measures change over time, and that the change in notability over time is as important as the notability itself. Something may be notable in one context but not in another. Or it may be mildly notable in one context but very important in another. The contexts may have relationships to one another, and the relationships may amplify or diminish the overall notability. In fact, this may be a separate issue; notability in the large may differ from notability in the small.

Some events are notable *and* indicative on their own without further correlations: one smallpox pustule suffices to garner a great deal of attention. Alternatively, an event may be notable not because it is unprecedented but because it suddenly appears more frequently, or, conversely, when unexpected (e.g., the dog that did not bark in Sir Arthur Conan Doyle's *Adventure of the Silver Blaze*). Some events are notable because of their context: an airplane passenger in beach attire. It may be notable that the president of a company otherwise reluctant to mingle with workers is spotted doing so several times over the course of a week. Mingling with other company presidents, however, may not be anomalous. An activity (e.g., someone casing a jewelry store) that cannot be explained *except* by reference to something troubling is itself notable. Finally, something may be notable to one person precisely *because* it is *not* notable to others: a newcomer may notice something funny ("why are there no black faces on this beach?") that others habituated to circumstances miss. Part of the problem is statistical significance in a nonstatistical domain. No one observer, on his or her own, will see enough to form statistically valid estimates (just as no parent raises enough children to form statistical estimates on what children are like); the hope, therefore, is that the various cases can be blended. But the solution of putting everything into a common bucket with a common classification methodology begs many questions and does nothing to focus human attention on the truly revealing outliers.

An important aspect of awareness is the recognition that one does not have all the dots. In the Belgrade example, planners were confident of their decision, in large measure, because they thought they had all the relevant (and correct) information at their disposal.[6] In retrospect (and these things are always more obvious when looking back), there were algorithms that planners could have used to force themselves to solicit more information. In other words, they should have known what they did not know (or at least know with sufficiently warranted confidence). Such a logic train would have run thus:

---

[6] Since the Kosovo campaign, the U.S. military has paid a great deal more attention to checking and rechecking no-strike lists. The fact remains, however, that list-checking is not considered glamorous and is likely to be assigned to those unable to get better tasking. Thus, energetic diligence to potential mistakes may not necessarily follow otherwise good intentions.

1. Besides losing a pilot, the worst thing a bombing run can do is hit a controversial target;
2. Among the most controversial targets are embassies;
3. Among the most sensitive embassies is China's; and
4. Therefore, one should make very sure that China's embassy is located correctly—so sure, in fact, that the U.S. National Imagery and Mapping Agency (NIMA) map that depicts the embassies should be scrubbed to see whether it is up-to-date (the Chinese embassy having moved just recently).

At that point, the planners could have broadcast a map of Belgrade to the U.S. international affairs community, saying: Is this a correct list and location of all the critical buildings, the striking of which would be very bad? Presumably, at least one U.S. consular official or defense attaché who had recently been posted to Belgrade (and thus potentially with enough interest in the matter to seriously scrutinize the target lists) would have responded with corrections. But again, one has to know that there is a potential problem—both with the risks as well as with the information one is working with—to inquire further. By contrast, there were few ways for U.S. officials posted in Belgrade to have anticipated the event, because they were not connected to the relevant military operations.

Awareness is communicative. One must know when to collect more information, and sometimes one has to be systematic about doing it. Conversely, as with disease surveillance, one may distinguish awareness that something is noteworthy from a further awareness that it should be brought to the attention of others.

Symmetric and asymmetric cases require a different sense of awareness. In the symmetric cases, people must be aware when they have information *needed by* others. In asymmetric cases, people must also be aware that they *need* information *from* others.

Lack of Attention

Attention puts information into play. *Attention* is the flip side of awareness; it gives information its due regard. That is, once you are aware of a dot's existence and importance, you pay attention to it and take action. Consider the Belgrade example and ask what it would have taken to get people to pay attention to the possibility of an inadvertent strike on a sensitive site. After all, NATO warplanes hit several thousand strike-points that spring. Past some point, most people whose jobs were other than vetting strike packages may well have tuned out to the repeated inquiry. Those who plan strike packages might not have gotten the message in time, might not have placed credibility in the source of the warning, might not have understood the nature of the warning, and so on. As Claude Shannon noted, noise (random misreading of bits) and bias (nonrandom misreading of bits) can interfere with all communications (Shannon, 1948). One can also imagine the reverse. Given a chance to comment on target lists, there may have been those in the embassy who would have taken exception to a great number of targets for political or humanitarian reasons. After a while, the target planners would have tuned *them* out, although a message saying, "Stop! Your maps are wrong. That's the Chinese embassy!" would still have garnered attention.

It has been suggested that a lot of information is always better than a little. But trying to pay attention to everything makes it more likely that nothing will get adequate attention. For example, no doctor has the time to read every report of every unusual disease condition, and no intelligence officer can read every update on any possible item related to the country or issue that she tracks. Thus any dot collection mechanism ought to have some way of downplaying information that should not get attention. The Pearl Harbor case illustrates that there was a high degree of cognizance that more information was needed. There was also a general willingness to be alert to any clues that were indicative. Thus, in the Pearl Harbor case, there was a great deal of awareness but very little attention paid to significant information. In such cases, a new factor can be introduced: the ambient noise level. That is, the information's notability must pass a threshold before action is considered.

The value of controlling noise is emphasized by Charles Peters in an article describing problems at the Central Intelligence Agency: "One reason that cables are not read is that too many of them are sent and too many are distributed to too many people. The truly important messages are buried amongst the travel itineraries of colleagues, statistics on the annual rainfall in Zimbabwe, and other such odds and ends that you don't need or want to know. The system of distribution and accountability desperately needs reform so that people get only the cables that are truly relevant to their work and then are held accountable for reading them." (Peters, 2002, p. 5)

At Pearl Harbor, having put themselves on alert several times earlier (notably in mid-1940), planners implicitly required that evidence pass a threshold. But the threshold was higher by the time the Japanese attacked. Although the noise level was probably not a result of deliberate Japanese actions, it could have been. (For example, in a similar circumstance, Egypt deliberately ran repeated exercises prior to the October 1973 war so that attack preparations were more easily dismissed by Israel.)

Attention is also subject to many influences. One is "pluralistic ignorance," where a group member knows or believes something, others know or believe the same thing, but no one member is aware that the others share the same knowledge or belief. A second is the inattention generated by differences in status among those who are communicating what to whom. That is, the hierarchy (formal or informal) can encourage or discourage when attention is paid. It takes a certain degree of status to get one's concerns recognized by others; recognition by a higher-up of an issue raised by someone in the ranks also confers status. Since status contention is ever-present in bureaucracies (although it plays differently in less flat as opposed to more flat organizations), this consideration has to be factored in.

Misuse of Templates

As noted earlier, *templates* are generalized patterns drawn by people from their experience to help them understand new situations (Klein, 1998). They are a means by which dots are put in context. This use of templates raises important questions about how to train novices and convert them to experts. For example, a large amount of medical training is based on case studies (the source of templates). Should the general success of such medical training suggest that terrorist experts be trained using case studies? And without sufficient exposure to a large number of cases, will useful templates be developed?

The answer is far from clear. Templates can obscure as well as enlighten, resulting in ignorance of what, in retrospect, should have been obvious. Templates can be involved in three kinds of errors: using the wrong template, not using a template when one exists, and not having a template for a given situation. To see how, consider the following examples.

Although people *were* worried about terrorism, they lacked templates specific to what happened on September 11. Circa mid-2001, the FBI was cautioned against profiling people based on their background (and so discounted the fact that the anti-American pilots-in-training were Arab). They were also reluctant to get search warrants based on Foreign Intelligence Surveillance Act (FISA) (counterintelligence) grounds, and so refused requests to submit Moussaoui's possessions to a more thorough search. After September 11, 2001, the sensitivity to harbingers of terrorism rose substantially, but the distribution of greater attention here inevitably comes at the expense of less attention elsewhere. (In the FBI's case, it was counterdrug operations.) Conversely, suppose someone had put out a general warning for the FBI to be alert for Arabs planning to hijack airlines and fly them to populated areas. (Again, these things are always easier to identify in retrospect.) With a warning like that—even if this warning had been one among, say, a hundred different warnings—it is likely that the agents in both Minneapolis and Phoenix would have sounded warning sirens and that people would have paid attention. Had this been the top priority warning, one such incident would have sufficed. Were the source of the anthrax-laden letters to be found, one can guarantee that someone would then discover anomalies that should have pointed to the source. But not every anomaly or unexplained event necessarily does. Thus, there must be more to a solution than merely ringing alarm bells.

The (hypothetical) disease surveillance example brings up similar issues. Doctors have templates for most conditions they encounter. But doctors recognize that the great variability among humans means that many people's conditions are unique but not necessarily interesting for that reason. Indeed, the variability among humans makes it difficult to know whether atypical symptoms are characteristic of atypical people or atypical diseases.[7] The physician's rule of thumb is to look for the more typical or average case first; it is often expressed as "if one hears hoofbeats, look for a horse first, rather than a zebra." Doctors mentally catalog these typical situations as templates; then they use the templates when deciding which of several diseases is the most likely one, based on symptoms, history, and context. The difficulty of accurate diagnosis is compounded when familiarity suggests one template when in fact another may be more appropriate. Sometimes, such as with the outbreak of SARS, the template misled only for a short time; the medical community swiftly recognized that it was dealing with a new phenomenon. But at other times, as with the anthrax cases, rigid adherence to a template may have prevented doctors from recognizing a new disease until people had died unnecessarily.

In theory, the incentives for checking for unusual phenomena, if only to rule them out, should increase more than proportionately, for two reasons. First, unusual events may be more likely today, if only because the more complex nature of our society makes it difficult to understand interactions and anticipate events. Second, early detection of unusual events may save lives well beyond those of the immediate patients presenting the odd symptoms. But an increased emphasis on checking can backfire, either by eating up valuable time or by desensitizing the checker; there's the boy who cried wolf once too often.

Clearly, in the case of the Beltway sniper, the template was defined too soon, and thus unexpected information had little opportunity to be combined with what was already known. Profilers were out in force determining what neighborhood the snipers came from, and the police were looking for a white van; both were misled. Also in

---

[7] At least these days, the public health community has reason to be aware that any one case may be the harbinger of a new wave of unseen cases: (1) easier transportation, which permits exotic diseases to be carried far from their origins (global warming is also shifting diseases away from their historic habitat), (2) the growing resistance of pathogens to antibiotics, and (3) the threat of bioterrorism.

error was the behavioral assumption that the killers would be fleeing the scene of the shooting rather than staying behind (eating French fries), confident that they were not seen. The next template for such an attack may assume incorporation of a search for a pattern of unsolved crimes over the weeks and months previous. Whether such a template maintains its relevance the next time is anyone's guess.

There are only so many templates people can keep in their heads for any one[8] field or situation. The solution to our problem may require a structure that anticipates this inherent limitation, as well as the way in which experience biases recognition. We must take into account that when different communities view the same data, they match it against patterns that are organized in different ways. For instance, a chemist considering global warming is likely to note the chemicals, temperatures and pressures involved, while a biologist or anthropologist is likely to note the effects on wildlife or people. Similarly, differences in experience and background, combined with slightly different physical evidence, can yield wildly different interpretations of the same thing, as when seven blind men touch an elephant. As the story goes, because each takes a different perspective, they think they see seven different creatures. Had they shared their information, they might have discovered that all were dealing with an elephant. Understanding these differences in perception may help us to understand the best ways to assess a situation and communicate findings. We need to investigate what experts view in the same way, and where and when the differences arise.

The misuse of templates is related to the several ways that our problem can fail to be solved, as shown in Table 1.3. We can make mistakes by omission, as when a medical symptom is not recognized (not having a template). We can also make mistakes by commission, as when the wrong evidence became the focus of the sniper investigation (using the wrong template). We can also have a missed opportunity, as the Pearl Harbor vignette illustrates (not using the template).

---

[8] The *total* number of templates that anyone holds may be large if they span divergent domains, such as those for writing texts, teaching classes, doing research, or publishing papers.

Table 1.3
Relationship of Errors to Template Misuse

Error Type	Template Misuse
Omission	Not having a template
Commission	Using the wrong template
Missed opportunity	Not using a template

Understanding how the templates are created suggests further insights. Gary Klein (1998) has noted that experts use a set of mental metaphors to encapsulate their experience and form templates to which they compare current situations. This matching process is difficult, especially when familiarity suggests one template but another is more appropriate. As noted earlier, much of a doctor's training is based on case studies (the source of templates), but we do not know how broadly this instructional technique can be applied. How can terrorist experts, for instance, see enough cases to develop reliable templates? Even when templates exist and are valid in many situations, how do we know when the templates are relevant in a particular situation? In describing the decisions made as the debris of the World Trade Center was being cleared, William Langewische (2002) points out that much of the expertise thought to be vital was in fact useless, while other expertise was unexpectedly essential. For example, the medical support readied itself for casualties that never surfaced, because most victims were killed instantly and many were vaporized. At the same time, the maintenance staff who knew minute details about how the twin towers were constructed were the only ones who could help the emergency crews navigate through the wreckage. The nature of the situation was so different from what anyone would have anticipated that typical emergency scenarios simply did not apply. Instead, those typical scenarios could have led to increasing the danger, not mitigating it. Fortunately, such errors were caught and corrected quickly, but only because of the personalities involved.

Compartmentalization

Much of the previous discussion has emphasized the need not only to recognize that information may be important but also to share it with the people who need to know about it. The networks of Table 1.3 and the transformations in Figure 1.1 illustrate mechanisms that can enable such sharing. But sharing is often inhibited by *compartmentalization:* the tendency of subcommunities to keep information to themselves, often for reasons of security. How would air campaign planners have found the embassy official who knew Belgrade well enough? Openly broadcasting the intent to strike every target risks compromising missions. Even doing so within NATO is no guarantee; operational headquarters were not leak-proof. In situations like this one, it might be possible to determine a balance point, where those who would ordinarily not need to know a piece of information, once told of it, can be removed from a site before their knowledge does direct or indirect damage. By contrast, broadcasting a map of Belgrade's no-strike zones (absent those nominated on the basis of sensitive intelligence) would have told no one anything that could not have been easily guessed by someone who knew the city. So two more issues must be addressed: how to broadcast and to whom to broadcast.

Security issues played a mixed role in the pre–September 11 search for terrorists. The FBI is a community with a high degree of external suspicion (and no small degree of internal competition, which tends to erode the internal trust). Files on terrorism cases were restricted to colleagues in the office of the agent in charge of a case. Since September 11, to "connect the dots," terrorist files have been opened up for general circulation. By late 2002, the pendulum had swung back so that only specific agents working on a case could see such information. The FBI's security dilemma was brought into heightened relief by the discovery of Robert Hanssen's spying the same year the World Trade Center was struck. Yet no systematic analysis had been done on the costs and benefits of extended versus constricted sharing of case files.

The FBI is still wrestling with how to grant access to members of local police forces (e.g., the New York Police Department) as members of terrorism task forces. (The counterintelligence community struggles with the same problem; compartmentalized information is the norm, with projects and technology organized using strict barriers.) And the FBI's internal networks still have inadequate facilities for bringing information to the general attention of others. Agents are very case-oriented; they are less interested in general understanding than are their counterparts in intelligence agencies. This organizational culture must be embraced in any solution, so that trust and credibility are mapped into any process that supports decision-making.

The unexpected interaction between air bags and theft protection illustrates that compartmentalization can occur even where security factors are not paramount. Indeed, the social science literature suggests that people tend to compartmentalize naturally, to break problems into smaller elements that are more manageable and understandable. But, as when blind men independently describe an elephant, this tendency can mislead; the compartmentalization restricts context and excludes critical evidence.

The seven examples offer many instances of the barriers we describe; the mapping of examples to barriers is made explicit in Table 1.4. Additional examples are offered daily in newspaper

Table 1.4
Correlating Barriers to Examples

	Awareness	Attention	Templates	Compartmentalization
9/11 terrorism	✓	✓	✓	✓
Diseases	✓		✓	
Beltway sniper	✓		✓	
Pearl Harbor		✓	✓	✓
Embassy bombing	✓			✓
Car manufacturing	✓			✓
Challenger		✓		✓

articles and historical analyses. These additional instances will enrich our understanding not only of these barriers and the possible approaches to overcoming them, but also of other barriers of which we are not yet aware. Thus, the next step in our investigation is to model some of what we understand to explore the implications of change.

CHAPTER TWO

Modeling Communication of Information

To understand dot collection and dissemination, it is important to understand how information circulates within an existing organization or community.[1] To enhance our understanding, we built a simple syncretic model that incorporates and tests basic assumptions about how the communication works.[2] Can small changes in the number of reinforcing dots improve the chance that such dots will collectively be seen as notable? The model tests this proposition:

> If we selectively circulate information about a phenomenon, we can increase the likelihood that the phenomenon will be recognized as significant (in some way) more often than through random circulation of information about the phenomenon.

The model works in the following way. First, a set of indications (that is, characteristics of the phenomenon) is scattered throughout a population of individuals. The phenomenon (hereafter called a "true fact") is associated with slightly more characteristics than the rest (hereafter called "false facts"). As individuals are excited by the information they have, they tell their friends. If the friends, in turn, are excited about the information they have (a combination of what they

---

[1] In this discussion, we assume that the community has already been formed. Although this may be a naive assumption, it reflects the fact that there are already established communities unable to collect and connect dots. We address this partial problem first; once it is solved, we are happy to turn to the broader problem of creating appropriate communities to address key issues.

[2] This model, in Visual Basic, is available on request.

were given originally and what they heard from others), they tell their friends, and so on. After several rounds, if a phenomenon's unusual characteristics pass a predetermined threshold, the phenomenon is reported as significant. The model's results suggest that such circulatory mechanisms can, in fact, raise the odds that collecting the dots can point to a phenomenon with an unusual set of characteristics.

Thus, the model suggests that any solution must monitor not only the dots but also their characteristics and the way in which the dots and characteristics are communicated from one person or organization to another. This key finding is the core of what we envision as an approach to solving the dot collection problem. In the next section, we describe in more detail what a potential solution might involve.

CHAPTER THREE
Elements of Potential Solutions

The concepts, barriers, and frameworks described earlier suggest some of the elements of collecting and communicating dots, but far from all. They provide a starting point from which we can describe what a more complete solution might incorporate. What we seek ventures beyond general notions of the relationships among data, knowledge, and information; we must go beyond ontologies and organizing mechanisms to more active ways of enabling people to use information effectively. That is, we are looking not only for ways to identify information relevant to a problem, but also for ways to know how to find information that we suspect would be relevant if we had it, and to know when it is significant enough to require action. Underlying this search is the belief that several pieces of information in combination are often more powerful (in terms of importance) than the sum of their constituent parts. We seek to know both when to pay attention and also how to get the attention of others who may need to know what we have discovered. In a sense, the topic is dual: how to promote information-sharing and how to induce early detection, knowing full well that detection is only one reason for information-sharing and that many additional factors can improve detection.

In some ways, techniques to improve dot collection would be more effective if any or all of the explicit barriers to sharing information were explicitly addressed. In other ways, techniques such as automated information analysis may be employed to permit dots to be collected even in the face of such barriers.

A naive solution is sometimes attempted, based on the notion that information technology will sort through properly tagged items and find anomalies or relationships. To implement such a solution, a system would have to elicit all such facts (events, relationships, perceptions, etc.) and absorb them in a systematic, consistent way. Automation may or may not be part of a solution, but in an age when people are flooded with information (most of which they cannot use), there are no guarantees that automated systems will bring the dots together and organize them appropriately. Furthermore, even when automated systems can handle enormous volumes of data, there are real obstacles to capturing everything and doing so in a meaningful way.

More realistically, we look for a solution that reflects the multidisciplinary nature of the problem. That is, any solution we find is bound to mix both organizational and technological elements. The organizational elements include networking community members (in the social rather than electronic sense) and recognizing correct roles and responsibilities. Collaboration is a companion to the networking, combining organizational and technical elements in a way that enables people to function most effectively in identification and communication. At the same time, any solution must include some form of codification and categorization, so that the information gathered is labeled, organized, and stored in a way that makes it easy to find again and easy to associate with other, related information. Although codification and categorization are largely technical issues, they have sociological aspects as well, reflecting the ways that people recognize and combine disparate pieces to build a bigger picture. We explore each of these facets of a solution in turn.

Networking

The patterns of social networking have a great deal to do with how well information is circulated. Although electronic networking may be a sine qua non of sharing, it alone is not sufficient. Social networking is implicit in at least part of the solution, as much previous work has shown.

The matching of pieces of information, and especially of needs to knowns, requires that we know what techniques can accelerate the transfer of information from where it sits to where it is needed. Some sort of networking—both electronic and social—is clearly required for information transfer. The physical networking is fairly straightforward using information technology, and the associated network security concerns can be handled with a variety of tools and techniques. Table 1.1 illustrated the several kinds of networks needed; for each concern and context we can define, there is a community of interest involved in addressing that concern in that context.

In some cases, we can define the relevant social community, but in others the definition and boundaries of the community are not necessarily clear or even unambiguous and stable. A solution may begin with a less-well-defined community and then make it more specific, inclusive, or exclusive as more information is gathered. But any community that has a name is likely to have some existing social networking. The solution may in fact generate rules for refining the community definition. For example, one way to identify the communities or community members for inclusion is to identify objects of discourse that cross boundaries between groups.

But it is not enough to assume that we need networks once we find dots. We may also need to acknowledge the networks that lead up to information transfer. That is, social networking tends to *precede* the transfer of information. For example, finding a job is often a matter of mating two facts: someone's need for a job and someone's knowledge that there is an opening somewhere. Most people who find jobs through references tend to rely on social networking, particularly by using weak ties (of which there are many) rather than strong ones (of which each of us has few). In such cases, social networking is essential. Yet is the difference between job hunting and dot collecting/connecting merely one of scale? Yes and no. The medical community illustrates the duality of the problem. On the one hand, the U.S. medical community is large, even if limited to primary care and emergency room physicians, and it is still sizeable if scoped down to, say, the Washington, D.C., metropolitan area. So two randomly selected doctors are unlikely to know one another. On the other hand, all such doctors are professional peers of one another. They need no introductions to begin taking each other seriously; the network created by their shared education and skill connects them easily and quickly, lending them credibility and respect as well as instant access.

Moreover, the credibility and respect of the sender of information may in many ways color the way it is received, so that more attention is understandably paid to highly credible or known sources. That credibility can be amplified or dampened by our perceptions or biases; we bring our own biases to the table, intentionally or not. Moreover, the evaluation of credibility may not be straightforward; I may ignore a waiter with news of a job opportunity until I find out that the waiter is actually a retired worker in my field who likes to serve at his son's restaurant. Thus, an important part of making a piece of information visible is establishing or evaluating the credentials of the possible sources and even destinations of information.

The role of networking cannot be understated. We often rely on social networks to find facts and relay them to the appropriate receivers. Indeed, recent networking theory has emphasized the constructive role that may be played by people whose singular talent is that they know and are known by many people within an organization. These connectors help to enable social networking; they are like the busybodies that Jane Jacobs (1961) recommends as essential for a safe, healthy neighborhood. Their role involves not only mating people or entities who need to know each other's interests or information but also acting as early warning signals of anomalous but often ill-defined information or situations. A connector can, for example, notify the police of "strange activity" or "unusual circumstances"; it is the police who then clarify and amplify what is known.

A colleague of ours can be described as a connector. Because his antennae are attuned to marketing, he is quite able to connect the vague needs of several hundred potential customers with the capabilities of several hundred potential researchers. People talk to him because he is known as a potential broker; he is effective because he has ample information gathered from the people and organizations that communicate with him. To appreciate the role of such connectors, a key question must be answered: What does it take for connectors to realize the importance of what they hear? They too have to filter out noise in order to pass along what they think someone else wants or needs to hear. To what type and volume of information do connectors actually react? Must they know how to receive and interpret what people are saying? Must they filter information or discard sources lacking in credibility? Is their role to monitor the word on the street or to filter that word through a screen of perceived needs? And when does the filter prevent important information from passing through? That is, would someone attuned to one goal (e.g., increasing marketing opportunities) necessarily see relevance to another (e.g., opportunities to develop new forms of multidisciplinary inquiry)? For instance, it takes a special talent to recognize that a concept arising from health policy has application to military planning.

Finally, understanding the connection in a network means understanding how pieces of information contribute to the overall body of evidence that is gathered. It may be that only certain forms of connection are self-reinforcing. Other connections may attract irrelevant information, or worse—information that confuses or obfuscates the real message. These issues can be understood by investigating the roles and responsibilities of the members of a network or set of networks.

Roles and Responsibilities

Networking is a social phenomenon that typically extends beyond organizations. But within a given organization, each constituent person or group can be identified by roles and responsibilities. There are at least three types of roles in any process that addresses our problem: decisionmakers, perceivers, and connectors (where any given person may play more than one role). Decisionmakers are people or organizations that must investigate the dots, their meanings, and their relationships to make decisions on behalf of their organizations. The dots act as pieces of evidence, and decisionmakers evaluate the evidence, a set of possible actions, and the case made for each option using the evidence at hand. These decisions can take place within a given organization or among organizations, where people in the organization produce or find the evidence and sometimes construct the case for one or more options. That is, the decisionmakers act in response to actions taken by other actors in the organization.

Perceivers see that some event or fact is notable in some way, and they may or may not notify others (decisionmakers, connectors, other perceivers) of the existence of the notable action. The perceivers thus associate some degree of credibility with the evidence that is provided to the decisionmakers.

As noted above, connectors are those who keep track of the other two roles, knowing when it is appropriate to make known to one group or person a notable event highlighted by a perceiver. Of course, a single individual can take on multiple roles, especially at different times during a process or activity.

Networks depend on communication among all roles. This communication can take at least two forms. One is the communication among the participant types. We can ask how perceivers communicate among themselves, how connectors communicate among themselves, and so on. The second is communication across participant types. How do connectors communicate their findings to relevant parties? What is the role of synchronous versus asynchronous communication?

We may be able to express the communications among roles in different ways. Participant A may communicate regularly with participant B to exchange one category of information (such as work-related information) but only sporadically with participant B in another category (such as personal information). For example, suppose A and B work together and are keen cyclists. They may exchange work information in one network of colleagues, but also exchange cycling information in a separate but related network of colleagues (assuming their work is not in the cycling business). Thus, the context helps to determine the nature, mechanism, and frequency of communication. In this sense, the roles and responsibilities may change with the context. Moreover, the mechanisms may also be different depending on context; the work information may be expressed in memos and personal communication, while the cycling information may be exchanged in phone calls and e-mail.

Once roles are identified, who is responsible for identification (including matching needs to knowns) and notification? For example, doctors seem to be individually responsible and occasionally motivated to participate in this process (although public health infrastructures exist in awareness that such intracommunity efforts are not enough). The FBI example defers this responsibility to senior management rather than field agents. In the Belgrade example, both the consular corps and the planners were stakeholders in the outcome, but neither seemed to understand the responsibility for matching. Indeed, this situation provides an example of the effects of an informal hierarchy and its dampening effect; the planners probably viewed consular officials as potential security leaks, so there was a disincentive to share (while former defense attachés, once assigned elsewhere, may not have had sufficient need-to-know to get inside the circle).

Similarly, we need to know who has responsibility for each of these actions: identifying the knowledge, making sure it is correct, deciding to whom to broadcast it, getting feedback, and ensuring the correctness of the feedback. There are examples of second-rank pilots failing to do what was necessary to stop disasters because the chief pilot either did not listen to them or the relationship was such that the second-level officer did not speak out. These steps in turn may require iteration and expansion, so knowing when to stop—when we have enough information of the relevant kind—is another issue to be addressed, as is the issue of which communication model is the most effective in a given situation. For example, without paying attention it might not have been obvious even to someone who knew where the Chinese embassy was that what was labeled as the home of a supply bureaucracy was in fact an embassy.

To address these issues, a solution might introduce organizational incentives to improve fact-mating, including creating incentives for people to share information. If this aspect is an essential ingredient in the solution's recipe, then the cultures of many intelligence and law-enforcement communities explain why difficulties have been encountered in them in the past. In these communities, where sharing information would seem to be critical, it is in fact the protection and hoarding of information that is rewarded. For example, the FBI is infamous for not sharing its information with local law enforcement organizations, because agents get credit for cases they crack. Similarly, the intelligence community has less-pronounced incentives exacerbated by strict need-to-know rules and a culture that attracts people who like to know facts precisely because the facts are not known by others.

Yet not all restrictions are based on security needs. There is a tendency for people faced with complex and potentially controversial decisions to compartmentalize, limiting discussions to principals and throwing everyone else out of the room. But when dealing with complex systems (especially in the asymmetric case), it is important to bring into play those people with arcane knowledge on the possibility that one of them will say: Did you know that the consequence of doing X (e.g., bombing the aforementioned building in Belgrade, or launching in cold weather) is that variable Y (e.g., relations with the Chinese, or the stability of O-rings) will become critical?

Any approach to effective dot collection must also acknowledge the number and kinds of disparate information that can be tracked at one time. In many milieux, such as in newsrooms, among market analysts, or at guard stations, people have demonstrated an ability to watch more screens simultaneously than was thought possible. To devise a dot collection approach, there must be some way for people to enter into multiple collaborations simultaneously for the explicit purpose of piping up when something seems to be going awry in their specialty.

It is also important to acknowledge that not all decisions are of equal weight or importance. A dot collection system must be explicit about what sorts of decisions need to be made, the issues raised by these decisions, and the implications if the decision is less than optimal. However, over-analysis can impede useful decisionmaking. To see how, consider the activities of a team designing a new car (Kleiner and Roth, 2000, p. 147). The team decided to document a much wider array of potential problems (than was normally considered) to determine what might impede the on-time introduction of a new model. This approach enabled everyone on the team to review a variety of factors and to determine each factor's impact on their own work. Unfortunately, the simple tally of adverse factors was much higher than what might have been expected in standard practice; the number of potential problems was inflated by anticipating problems instead of waiting for them to be revealed. This situation suggested to some managers that the new car team was in far worse trouble than its predecessors, even though the prediction exercise could have enabled the team to nip many problems in the bud. Although the extensive risk analysis painted a darker picture than usual, the explicit documentation of how each system component's parameters might affect the behavior of other components was invaluable in suggesting who should be in touch with whom. This exercise in anticipation and interaction may be an essential part of any long-term solution to dot collection. In particular, in the symmetric case, prior relationships may be guessed through an explicit and imaginative development of templates that attempt to estimate what a set of significant causes may produce in the way of unexplained precursors or events.

Collaboration

Collaboration is a natural outgrowth of networking. Techniques of collaboration play an important role in ensuring that interactions among people who hold dots can progress in ways that reveal the relevant ones to those people and organizations that need to know about them.

In this instance, web and other information technologies may be helpful. Specific collaboration may also be useful in enabling users to examine what they know and to find related information. But the users are highly constrained by their communities and context, and organizational principles such as ontologies can act to restrict rather than liberate. In the examples discussed earlier, a common but significant problem is less one of getting two people to merge their knowledge and more one of getting the right two people together in the first place. Collaboration tools are available on the market and in research laboratories, but they rarely indicate with whom someone should collaborate. The canonical problem of figuring out who down the hallway knows something that can shed light on something that is bothering you is an inherently difficult one. Recent work on referential databases that contain information on who knows what provide limited help in this context, particularly for complex problems and situations where there is significant personnel turnover or large numbers of personnel (Carley and Schreiber, 2002).

A related challenge is getting people to share information that they hold uniquely. Research by Strasser and Dietz-Uhler (2001) suggests the latter may be tougher than it appears. In one experiment, certain facts (those favorable to a candidate) were distributed to all, but other facts (those unfavorable to a candidate) were distributed only to one or another person. The former were brought up in conversation much more often than the latter. Thus the conversation yielded an overall favorable impression of the candidate even though the weight of all facts combined would have indicated otherwise. The effect was vitiated—but only partially—when participants were told that, as a result of the specific facts they held, they could consider themselves "expert" on one or another facet of the candidate.

Mechanisms are needed to overcome the reluctance to share unique information. The reluctance can be particularly acute when the information that is being shared is risky or unfavorable to some. And even when there is no risk, perspective can block out as well as enlighten, as when each of the seven blind men characterized the elephant differently. In a solution to dot collection, information manipulation (and those skilled at doing it) may be just as important as the pieces of information themselves. But if what the manipulators see is determined only by where they stand, reliance on reputation or perspective can be meaningless or worse.

It may also be important for each person to focus on anomalies. The more independent from the whole is each person's thinking, the greater the odds that someone can put together a set of disparate clues in new and potentially correct ways. But it is possible that such independence may make it less likely that one person can elicit from another the dots that make a complete picture. And if these connections depend on mental models that differ from one person to another, no one categorization will work for all situations. Given the current state of systems development, collecting and connecting dots is something that is likely to require brainpower more than faster CPUs.

Categorization

The ability to categorize information properly increases the likelihood that two pieces of relevant information will be mated appropriately. Consistent categorization can help machines to help people connect the dots that are most logically related to one another. However, inappropriate categorization schemes can hinder. For example, many libraries have changed from the Dewey decimal system to the Library of Congress system, because the latter is more suitable for browsing related topics. Similarly, Prieto-Díaz and Freeman (1987) argue that faceted classification schemes are preferred to hierarchical ones for organizing repositories of software components.

Even when the categorization is useful, the underlying concepts and perceptions of importance must be consistent and visible. In particular, because they differ in what they think merits note, people may not necessarily learn much by exchanging information with one another in the absence of clear connections drawn among the issues they find important.

Categorization on a large scale is daunting, in part because the possible number of connections can be computationally unwieldy as well as difficult to depict to the person or system who wants to match up two or more items. We can simplify the problem by considering it in small chunks. Such binning can help sort out the number of people who have an interest in something because it is somewhere (so they are more likely to know one another). It also limits the information that needs to be circulated (compared to all information for a battlefield) and so more attention will be paid to any one fact. In other words, rather than trying to find two matching pieces in a big pile, one separates the big pile into n smaller piles on the assumption that the two matching pieces will end up themselves in the same small pile. Even if one does not know which pile, finding matching pieces in n piles is a problem of magnitude in the order of n; finding them in the combined pile is an n^2 problem.

The most obvious binning—especially for defense issues—is geospatial. For example, intelligence analysts sometimes use geography as the construct around which to organize existing intelligence (e.g., signals intelligence or unmanned autonomous vehicle imagery). This use of geography as an organizing principle enables the analysis to be done under tight operational and time pressures. Thus, the value of the binning is much more than simply enabling mapping.

Similarly, military planners think in terms of what's where and when because combat operations take place in confined locations (and because precision weapons rely on precision location information). But geospatial binning has its limits even in military domains. Many warfighters have only episodic interest in an area (such as when they are about to pass through it) and thus have little history to provide context for information content and flow. Geospatial binning may interfere with seeing phenomena that are related through other relationships. Consider, for instance, how the persistent use of maps depicting who controlled which territory hurt rather than helped in understanding the nature of the Vietnam War. (At the very least, control on both sides was contingent on time of day; some areas were under government control by day and Communist control by night.) So how to map facts a priori is not so obvious at the beginning of a situation or even straightforward later on.

In defense planning, everything is location, location, and location, but in the world of law enforcement, the watchwords are identity, identity, identity. Here we may have to bin by identity and personal relationships. Thus, another aspect of our more general problem is finding the best characteristic(s) to use as a basis for reducing the problem (or one of its aspects) to make it more tractable. And yet, when sorting information, many data points can belong in multiple groups. Consider, for example, the Beltway sniper incident. Did the Tarot card (found near Benjamin Tasker Middle School, where the sniper shot a student) belong with forensic clues, psychological profiling, or negotiation strategy? Here, it is not enough to decide on an organizing principle (such as hierarchy or faceted classification); evaluating and assigning the right (perhaps multiple) descriptive tags is critical.

It is instructive to examine the sniper example in more detail. Everyone who focused on the Beltway sniper knew that one, or at worst a few, vehicles were involved; there was one or at most two identities. But the heart of the problem involved associating a car sighting with an identity; no pre-binning would have offered much help. When the categories are concepts, binning is even harder. Of what is taking flight classes an example? How would one bin such an observation? There is also a thin line between taking advantage of geographic binning and being so wed to regional disaggregation as to miss clues that cross boundaries. Consider the methods of law enforcement officials in the United States. Here, states and localities usually act on their own. The state boundaries are often not helpful for information flow, and they can even prevent it. For instance, authorities in Atlanta did not consider the sniper incident there to be related to the ones in D.C. and Maryland. The fact that cars can move so easily across state borders is a problem, since the record of the car is kept within a single state. The same is true of drivers' licenses, still the main source of identification in the United States. Had a national registry of cars and owners existed, it would have been possible to search the registry's database for a blue Capri of a certain vintage. This search probably would have resulted in several thousand matches, helpful nevertheless because many people commit crimes near to their homes.[1] Thus, we may need tools that encourage us to modify our mental models or to create new mental models that suggest new hypotheses.

---

[1] The cross-border problem varies from region to region. The United Kingdom keeps all of its motor vehicle information in a central repository in Swansea, Wales. But the cross-border problem arises again when vehicles travel across European Union country boundaries. Similarly, even if the United States had had a central repository for motor vehicles (no matter the state), crossing borders would have been a problem if the car had been driven to Canada or Mexico.

The problems of categorization can also be addressed directly. Some researchers feel that a solution can be approached by defining a common set of terms to describe things in consistent ways. Using these terms, perhaps in concert with an encoding scheme such as XML (the extended markup language used for World Wide Web applications), similar facts and their features can be described so that machines can understand them to be the same. The hope is that if everyone contributes enough facts (or at least hunches) to some machine, the machine can then algorithmically mate them, find correlations, and expose significant anomalies more quickly and with greater capacity than can people. One appeal of this approach is that, ideally, it would obviate the social engineering required in enabling disparate individuals to communicate meaningfully with one another.

However, this approach faces many significant obstacles. One is getting people to note their facts (and hunches) in a diligent and consistent manner. For example, the system's utility is reduced if one person enters information daily but another enters it weekly; the mating may be delayed until it is no longer relevant. Another obstacle is the need for standards by which such facts are described; associated with this problem is the need for people to use such standards correctly. In both cases, the hard part is not so much denotation as definition; it is far easier, for instance, to standardize on the word "troubled" rather than "concerned" or "worried" than it is to have everyone define "troubled" in the same exact way. Multiple languages may add to the difficulties, as may multiple uses of the same word in different contexts or cultures. (For example, "tabling an issue" at a meeting in England has the opposite meaning of the same phrase in American English.) While standards may be set for ensuring that "tomahto" is understood as "tomato," they are less good (or even counterproductive) if applied to make everyone put facts into the same perspective. The point of common situational awareness is not only that everyone is aware of the same things, but also that they see the same thing if they look in the same direction. It is less obvious that everyone needs to have the same "spatial" orientation in the first place.

A related challenge is the ability to categorize new things—and anomalies are, by their nature, particularly likely to be "new." Phenomena are forever overstepping our attempts to categorize them. For instance, previous ethnic and racial distinctions are blurring in many cases. (Is Tiger Woods African-American or Asian-American?). A third challenge is making the correlation engine work. These obstacles may not be overcome in useful ways. Artificial intelligence holds some promise, but it may be too much to hope that it can discern fine shades of meaning or note meanings in context (such as "lead" the element and "lead" the verb). By contrast, people can be very good at seeing relationships among facts before they have explicitly determined the optimal set of rules for evaluating these relationships. Thus, it is likely that the categorization aspects of any solution to dot collection may involve humans interacting with an automated system to perform or refine the categorization.

Hybrid Approaches

In general, a human-machine hybrid may work better to collect the dots than a strategy that relies solely on social networking unaided by cognitive tools. Similarly, the installation of cognitive tools may be insufficient if it ignores the social dimensions of information-gathering.

For example, a hybrid approach might focus on asking people to carefully and completely report information to a central repository; then an automated system might assign people to seek relationships through some process that involves further interaction with machines. In fact, a more decentralized approach could take advantage of a human's keen pattern-recognition prowess. After identifying perceivers and connectors, an automated system could then rely on inducing the right person-to-person contacts as a way of getting facts to mate with one another. Here, technology can be used to facilitate the circulation of news of various types, including hunches and hypotheses as well as facts and relationships.

Many of the features of the Internet (such as Web sites, instant messaging, listservs in general, and David Farber's 25,000-strong "interesting-people" listserv) facilitate the circulation of news. That they flourish suggests that someone perceives some good from them. But the essential problem has not gone away: How can a source of facts be channeled so that each user gets what he or she needs (as defined by the problems they are solving)? Many attempts have been made to filter and refine the flow of news stories so that they better meet user requirements, but such an effort is nothing but a modest improvement over what came before. It is also unclear whether specificity is all that useful; the phenomena that call for fact-mating are, by their nature, unusual ones. Serendipity has a way of being serendipitous.

Combinatorial analysis and social science tell us that developing a denser set of person-to-person contacts yields an n^2 problem that does not scale well. Increasing the number of contacts (or actualizing existing ones) may leave people spending most of their time communicating instead of analyzing and reaching conclusions (Burt, 1992). This situation promotes "information stealing" (Burt, 1999) and group-think, thus mitigating the value of connections (Carley and Hill, 2001). We can ameliorate this problem by binning (as noted above) by using referential technology and by using gatekeepers or connectors to reduce the conversational overhead. Yet, the more layers we employ, the more we need communication among the connectors; if the system's architecture is not carefully defined, we may be trading a dense network of participants for a dense network of connectors. In fact, strong ties may be unnecessary; we may be able to rely on weak ties to communicate information. Thus, we should consider how altering the architecture of an organization affects what information gets circulated. Within a large information-gathering enterprise, different people may look at information with different filters, each trying to catch anomalies in his or her field. But too many things may be classified as anomalies. Overspecialization may reduce the ability to correlate facts that appear in different areas (one terrorist organization but in different regions; warnings of attack as they appear in diplomatic and military milieux).

An emerging branch of graph theory is known as "small worlds," in which dense networks are peppered with a few people known primarily for knowing others (Watts and Strogatz, 1998; Watts, 1999). This field of study may prove illuminating. In a small world, one role for designated participants is to connect those people with an interest in the same facts. Matchmaking is not easy; matchmakers must not only spend enough time maintaining and expanding their sets of acquaintances and connections, but also be current enough in fields of interest to make efficient matches or know how to get such matches made. One difficulty here is that such people tend to have high cognitive load (Carley and Ren, 2001) and, though they serve as emergent leaders (particularly in distributed networks), they are also key targets whose removal from the overall network is likely to minimize its adaptability (Carley, 2002a).

Defining Solution Frameworks

We can put these elements together to form a framework for a possible solution. The framework in turn is the basis for a process that is hybrid in nature; humans perform some of the activities, while other steps are automated. The framework includes the four aspects discussed above: networking, roles and responsibilities, collaboration and categorization. Table 3.1 shows how each of these four addresses almost all of the barriers identified in analyzing the vignettes. In combination, the solution's elements tackle the key problems experienced in typical situations.

Table 3.1
A Framework for Addressing Barriers with Solution Elements

Solution Elements	Barriers			
	Lack of Awareness	Lack of Attention	Misuse of Templates	Compartmentalization
Networking	✓	✓	✓	✓
Roles and responsibilities	✓	✓	✓	✓
Collaboration	✓	✓	✓	✓
Categorization	✓		✓	✓

The formal process's role for human expertise should include heuristics for recognizing patterns and relationships based on experience and knowledge. Figure 3.1 suggests a possible framework that includes five essential subprocesses and incorporates the roles discussed earlier. It is an example of how the problem can be analyzed in parts; the technology and research available to support each subprocess varies, with some aspects easily implemented today and others requiring substantial new research.

Each subprocess aims at answering an overriding question, as shown on the right side of the box, while using one of the four solutions elements (networking, roles and responsibilities, collaboration, and categorization), as shown on the left side of the box. The human within each box represents the need for human interaction at each stage. Perceivers, decisionmakers, and communicators may be active in each subprocess, but there is a dominant player for each step. For example, the In-Box Monitor assists the perceiver in answering the question "What do we know?"

At the same time, each subprocess can be viewed in terms of the barriers it attempts to overcome, as shown in Table 3.2. The subprocess addresses detailed questions the answers to which make visible first whether the information is notable and second whether it is credible and should be communicated to others. For this reason, the lack of awareness addressed by the In-Box Monitor is different from that of the Communicator; the latter informs others of some notable or useful piece of information.

This framework ties together the various concepts suggested not only by the literature but also by our analysis of the seven vignettes. By doing so, it suggests the steps that could be taken, using human-mediated automation, to discover a piece of notable information, evaluate it, and communicate it to those who should be aware of it. The framework assumes that there are mechanisms for obtaining information. Such an assumption is not unreasonable; each community has its ways of attracting and documenting facts, relationships, and events. Some automation already exists, in sensors, monitors, and gauges. We focus on understanding that information to determine whether it is a dot worth having and keeping.

Figure 3.1
A Framework for Recognizing and Communicating Notable Information

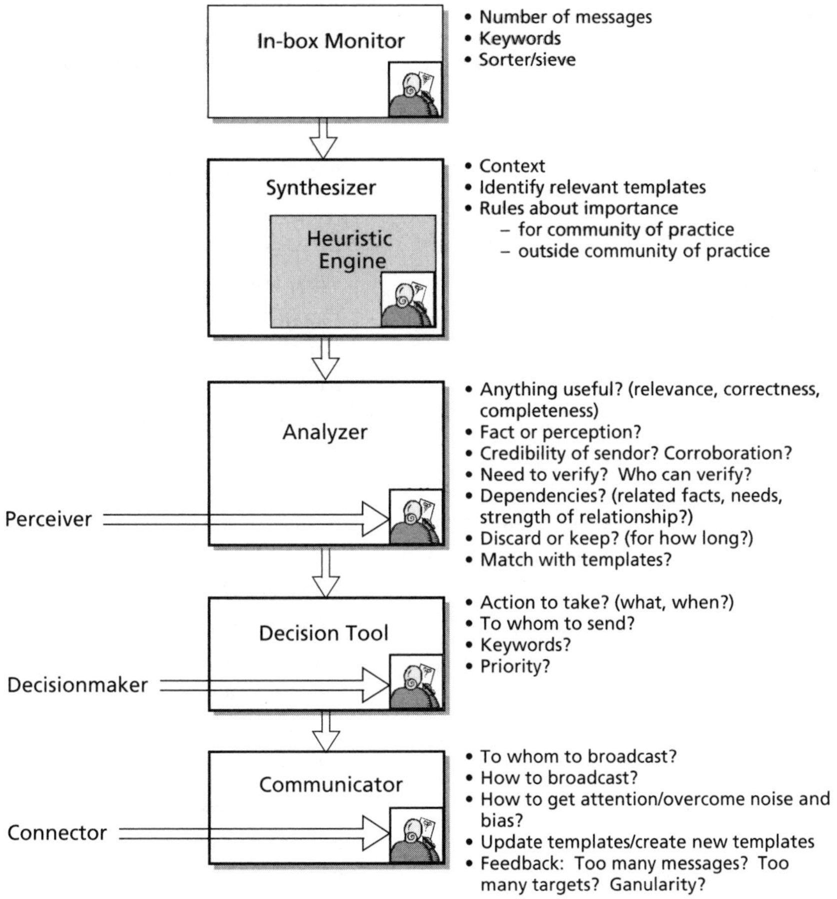

In-box Monitor	• Number of messages • Keywords • Sorter/sieve

Synthesizer
Heuristic Engine
	• Context
	• Identify relevant templates
	• Rules about importance
	  – for community of practice
	  – outside community of practice

Perceiver → **Analyzer**	• Anything useful? (relevance, correctness, completeness) • Fact or perception? • Credibility of sendor? Corroboration? • Need to verify? Who can verify? • Dependencies? (related facts, needs, strength of relationship?) • Discard or keep? (for how long?) • Match with templates?
Decisionmaker → **Decision Tool**	• Action to take? (what, when?) • To whom to send? • Keywords? • Priority?
Connector → **Communicator**	• To whom to broadcast? • How to broadcast? • How to get attention/overcome noise and bias? • Update templates/create new templates • Feedback: Too many messages? Too many targets? Ganularity?

RAND *OP103-3.1*

We describe each subprocess in turn.

In-Box Monitor

The first subprocess captures the information an individual or the community asks for or simply gets from other individuals or communities. This monitor can track the information in a variety of ways, such as messages, images or relationship diagrams. The information

Table 3.2
Detailed Questions Addressed by Each Subprocess

Subprocess	Barriers to Overcome	Questions
In-Box Monitor (What do we know?)	Lack of awareness	What are the nature and magnitude of the new information?
		How can we describe it?
		Should we apply a sort or sieve to improve visibility or meaning?
Synthesizer (What is the context?)	Misuse of templates	Do we know the context?
		What are relevant templates?
		Do we have rules about its importance:
		– For an individual?
		– For a particular community of practice?
Decision Tool (Is this worth knowing?)	Lack of awareness Misuse of templates	Is the received information notable:
		– Because of frequency?
		– Because of identity?
		Does the information contain anything useful in terms of:
		– Relevance?
		– Correctness?
		– Completeness?
		Is it a fact or perception?
		What is the credibility of the conveyor or sender? Do we have or need corroboration?
		Are there dependencies, such as related facts or needs? What is the strength of the dependence relationship?
		Does it match with templates?

Table 6—continued

Subprocess	Barriers to Overcome	Questions
Decision Tool (Is this worth knowing?)	Lack of attention Compartmentalization	Should we discard it or keep it? If keep, for how long, and in what fashion? Who would want to know about it? What priority should it have?
Communicator (Whom should we tell?)	Lack of awareness (of others) Lack of attention Compartmentalization	To whom should it be broadcast? How should it be broadcast: – To get attention? – To overcome noise and bias? Should templates be created or updated? Is there feedback: – Too much information? – Too many recipients? – Appropriate granularity?

may have associated descriptive material, such as keywords or pointers to related elements. It may not matter whether the associated elements are assigned automatically (e.g., using a program that assigns them based on context and content) or by hand (e.g., by an intelligence officer). What matters is that the In-Box Monitor can filter and sort incoming information so that it can be categorized and binned for easier handling. Filtering and sorting may be done entirely by humans or with automated assistance (much as the Kartoo search engine at www.kartoo.com allows users to fine-tune queries).

Synthesizer

A second subprocess synthesizes the messages by first establishing context(s) for information, again with various degrees of automation. Human experts then help identify candidate templates (retrieved from a database of stored templates) to explain the information in light of its context and nature. It adds information about relationships (including possible cause and effect) to help analysts determine whether multiple dots may be somehow connected. Then, using context and template together with the basic input, analysts can use a "heuristic engine"—a set of rules developed over time—to assess whether there are related rules about the importance of this information to an individual or particular community.

Analyzer

Preliminary assessments (perhaps more than one if different contexts or interpretations apply) are fed to a third subprocess, an analyzer. Its goal is to pick out related information that, when added to the new information, can help inform the bigger picture and decide if the received information is notable. Thus, this subprocess supports perceivers as they decide if something is interesting. Every component of this larger view is assessed to determine whether it is relevant, correct, and complete. Is it a fact or perception? How well does it correlate with what came before? Do others report the same or similar events, opinions, or observations? How credible is its source? Does it need to be verified, and if so, by whom? To determine how notable new information is, the analyzer must examine the dependencies among related pieces of information. It is here that needs and knowns may be matched. What are the related needs and facts? What are the strengths of relationships in this network of dependencies? With that, the analyzer can verify whether the information matches templates, usually by using its larger set of associated facts and observations. The broader the base of templates and contexts, the more effective the analyzer. Lack of breadth can seriously hamper the system's ability to make an appropriate choice.

Decision Tool

The fourth subprocess acts as an automated decisionmaker, interacting with the community's human decisionmakers. It uses the analyzer's designated sets of information and templates to determine and evaluate whether the information should be stored (and for how long), what priority it should have, and whether the information should be made visible to others. It is at this step that human decisionmakers use their skills in recognizing patterns.

Communicator

The output from the Decision Tool is fed to the fifth subprocess, the Communicator, which plays a connector role. It deals with audiences for what has been discovered, in the process finding good recipients and selecting communications methods. The success of the communicator is highly dependent on the degree to which the organization will delegate the role of "eyes and ears." This subprocess must also analyze its inputs and outputs to fine-tune communication based on what came before, such as the changing nature of needs and knowns. It may also create new templates to capture situations not previously experienced or understood. Feedback from other communities may lead to changes in the volume of information released, the granularity of information imparted, or the number or kind of targets considered as recipients.

Each of the five subprocesses entails considerable modeling and simulation, the results of which are fed to human experts to fine-tune the results and alter processes accordingly. For example, models like our syncretic model can be used by the Communicator process to determine the best way to impart information to others. Similarly, models can be built to match templates to information, or to evaluate the likely novelty of new input. At the same time, people are essential at each step, because they can perceive patterns that are not otherwise evident. Notions of similarity and difference (as in comparing a horse with a zebra) and evidence of possible relationships (as in connecting an embassy with a target list) may be added by humans where not otherwise identified automatically. Hunches, feelings, and subjective analyses (such as assessments of credibility) can be used to weigh and balance facts and observations, enriching models over time.

The framework can be applied within a community of practice, with communications among and across the subprocesses occurring as necessary. The processes themselves can loop and iterate among one another to accommodate lessons learned. In turn, a community of practice may implement the framework to communicate across communities, addressing barriers of compartmentalization and reducing bias.

The iterative nature of these processes may conflict with the hierarchical nature of some organizations. But the lack of hierarchy in the solution is key to its success. Each of the various communities is expected to talk to one another; the outputs of one are the inputs for others. This aggregate network must also be assessed and fine-tuned, and from several points of view. We must determine whether messages are sent from one community to another with the right kinds of information at the right level of granularity to the most appropriate people. Feedback on these characteristics can be generated automatically from simulations or measures of effectiveness, as well as manually, from humans who observe or participate in the process. When characteristics are out of balance (e.g., when some communities are overloaded with information or when the information is not given the right priority), the network must be rebalanced.

CHAPTER FOUR

Future Directions: Outlining a Solution

The framework we propose is necessarily skeletal. It awaits not only a more thorough investigation of many disciplines, including cognitive psychology and theories of social behavior, but also a better understanding of how to recognize a good solution. Moreover, this outline of a possible solution involves many pieces, each of which can be difficult to design and implement. Nevertheless, each piece is an essential part of a more comprehensive approach. As we learn more, each piece can be refined and expanded. In this section, we suggest how to proceed with designing and implementing a solution.

The proposed solution framework contains processes that address the key issues raised by our analysis. Before design can begin, one must first have a sense of how to recognize a good solution (whereas a "best" solution may be in the eye of the beholder). In the short run, we can apply the framework to our seven scenarios to determine if it would have helped or hindered in recognizing, assessing, and communicating information to avoid or mitigate the problems they represent. In the long run, we must acknowledge that the framework cannot be one-size-fits-all; it must be tailorable, so that it can be adjusted to address the particular needs of an individual, community, or set of communities.

Thus, we need to define a set of desirable qualities for such a framework and to monitor and improve these qualities over time. Typically, effectiveness and efficiency are initial goals for such an ambitious endeavor. An effective framework helps get the right information to the right people so that they can make a good decision; an efficient one does it without delay (or with acceptable delay). Effectiveness may be more important in one scenario, efficiency in another. So we need to find ways to formally express these criteria, balance them, and evaluate the likelihood of meeting them with a given solution.

To this end, we must ask:

- For a given solution, what kinds of things does the solution capture?
- What does it miss?
- Can this "hit rate" be improved?
- Can we use the solution structure and inputs received to assess the probability of capture of the right information? Of enough information?
- How can we characterize the set of satisfactory solutions? Is there a way to select an optimal solution?
- Acknowledging that we may very well have partial solutions, can we express and evaluate the degree of completeness of a solution?

To address these issues, we need a macroscopic view, wherein a model guides us in characterizing a proposed solution, evaluating the characteristics of the solution and the likely results, and providing the basis for the solution's implementation. It is likely that different solutions will be designed for different contexts, but consistency of design principles and notation schemes will enable disparate communities to communicate easily as needs arise—and as they may be forced to do quickly.

It is important to remember that the problem we address is key to national security, public health, and other essential aspects of American life. For this reason, any research agenda to address it must take careful steps to ensure that the proposed solution is one in which we can have a high degree of confidence. Thus, the research agenda must combine three elements:

- Ideas that evolve from observing and analyzing success and failure of past and current situations where such a solution could have been helpful;
- Incorporation of leading edge concepts from both information technology and social science (particularly those related to dynamic network analysis); and
- The fusion of human expertise with technological assistance.

We can reach our goal by organizing our activity in three steps. The first step is modeling the information processing characteristics of large organizations, focusing on their ability to detect and communicate indicative bits of information (that is, the dots). The second step involves developing tools to improve their enterprise- or community-wide situational awareness. The third and final step is to test these tools by comparing their results with the results of actual situations observed in the first step. We describe each of these activities in turn.

Step 1: Investigating Relationships, Parameters, and Metrics

The critical first step is to establish models of how an organization elicits and circulates information. The models depend on an understanding of what makes such information-gathering and dissemination successful; then, the nature and degree of success must be captured in metrics that can be compared and contrasted across different circumstances. The metrics might range from the ability to detect events or relationships that are quasi-routine (e.g., any piece of interesting information) to those that are somewhat out of the ordinary and merit some attention to those that are extraordinary and merit great attention. These metrics reflect the need for gradations of notability. They can be qualitative (e.g., moderately notable, highly notable), as long as they are consistently applied and contrasted.

Once the metrics are in place, models can be built to evaluate how well institutions elicit and circulate information. The model's parameters should have explanatory value, so that we can monitor progress and understand what to change in order to improve. The parameters will include a mix of external factors (e.g., the business an institution is in) and policy factors (e.g., deliberate choices made by this institution). This investigation would yield a framework for assessing a given institution or community's capability to collect the dots.

A key aim of the first part is to establish a working understanding of the proper mix of automated and organizational approaches to improvement. Placing a heavy emphasis on fieldwork would keep the results realistic and useful. This step, in turn, requires interviewing practitioners whose work requires them to collect, disseminate, and connect the dots. As relevant facts, relationships, communication mechanisms, roles, and responsibilities come into focus, the data models, requirement descriptions, and overall understanding of the process involved in identifying what is important and communicating it among those who need to know can all evolve accordingly. A proper initial focus is on a single community of practice.

Several issues—notably the nature of information at the human and data level—need to be explored to understand how well artificial intelligence can support these endeavors. At the human level, one must ask: How can decision processes be codified into a set of rules, given the type(s) of information available? Often, a small set of rules will provide a large amount of coverage. Of potential help are structures similar to Bayesian networks, decision graphs, and the various formalizations of causation, following the research of Jensen (2001), Pearl (2000), and Spirtes et al. (2000). Further, recent analyses concerning the "thinness" of results gotten by simply looking at the data (Brown and Duguid, 2000) argue that information should be analyzed using the logic of human cognitive activity, not just the logic of data exchange. Consequently, the rich field of logics of knowledge should be exploited to increase the analytic coverage (Fagin et al., 1995; Hintikka, 1962).

Exploring the data level requires modifying and using well-founded statistical methods to discover and exploit correlations between the low-level data streams and higher-level decisionmaking. Although basic rules may provide broad coverage, often the last 10–20 percent are the most difficult to capture in a rule-based system. Statistical artificial intelligence methods have proven extremely useful over the last decade at capturing this remainder, especially in such areas as statistical natural-language processing (Manning and Schutze, 1999; Jelinek, 1998; and Charniak, 1994). Fuller coverage could come from bridging these two types of methods. Combining these two types of artificial intelligence is an idea that is just beginning to take shape in the computer science community.

The completion of step one requires refining a working abstraction of information-sharing within communities by using heuristic models developed to test initial formulations. Completing the development of models of organizational relationships would create a context into which the various elements of our solution framework can be fit. The focus will be both on determining when a piece of information is deemed to be important and on how to communicate it to those who need to know it (and in a way that gets attention appropriate to the level of importance). It is important to define and build templates, to capture notions of relevance, and to measure characteristics such as need to know.

Modeling and simulation follow. It is first necessary to create methods by which institutions can characterize context (to help determine which facts are "notable"). Next, elements of a "marketplace" of awareness must be defined; in this marketplace, participants establish their needs so that the system can eventually match them with knowns. Criteria by which security and information-sharing can be balanced must also be developed, so that the matching generated by any system will respect the tension between these two parameters. The last activity in this step involves defining candidate procedures for annotating material with its appropriate level of interest. This step will include identifying organizational prerequisites for documenting interesting material so that it can be distributed to the people who need it.

The annotation of data for some specific purpose has become a fertile field of study in its own right. A key concern is developing an annotation scheme and data structures that allow for a rich enough data set, while being efficient enough to allow for tractable computation. That is, an annotation scheme must enable the system to describe a phenomenon in so detailed a fashion as to enable one phenomenon to be distinguished from another. But the descriptors cannot be so varied and numerous that the computational complexity becomes unwieldy or even infeasible. The Linguistic Data Consortium (http://www.ldc.upenn.edu) has datasets and tools developed to handle analogous problems in natural language processing and so can be a rich source of lessons learned.

Step 2: Designing Tools to Support Each Subprocess

The next step involves the initial design of the Analyzer, Synthesizer, and Communicator subprocesses, since these incorporate the most radical notions and thus the most risk. An understanding of information persistence is important in order to understand how long to retain information in a repository of possibly needed facts. The design of the three subprocesses will act as a reality check on the design of the other subprocesses, as we understand the interactions among all five. The current literature contains more information on the functions needed in the In-Box Monitor and Decision Tool, so the risk is lower in designing them. Models and simulations would help verify that the designs produce realistic results.

The questions in Table 3.2 provide the beginning of a set of requirements for each of the subprocesses. Traditional and well-known software engineering techniques can be used to elicit additional requirements. It is particularly important to instrument each process with the metrics described earlier, so that the results of modeling and simulation can be evaluated easily. That is, we want to be able to evaluate and tune the subprocesses, not only as we are designing and evolving the dot collection system but also in practice, so that we learn and improve as we use the tools.

Step 3: Implementing and Assessing the Tools

The third part of building a solution is testing its viability in actual situations. This step can be done by determining whether the solution works in situations where precursor events suggest ways to improve the situations rather than prevent them. We would begin by identifying in-house situations where researchers need to share information and be made aware of important or emerging data. Next, we would apply a suite of models to external sites with which we interacted in the first years of the study, with an emphasis on observing and interviewing members of the selected community of practice (e.g., the intelligence community) to see if they use and profit from the solution. Finally, we would repeat these tests in new communities, such as health or education, as they determine strategies for preventive health or learning interventions, respectively. Lessons learned from this stage of development will be fed back to the original heuristic models.

CHAPTER FIVE
Conclusions

To connect the dots you must first collect the dots. Much as we would like to assume that all those dots are out there awaiting connection, a brief assessment of a wide variety of examples suggests otherwise. Dots lie in disparate places and variegated files. Many never make it far from where they are created, so they are not known by those who need to be aware of their existence. Much of what is known in this world is carried in the heads of others and never committed to any permanent medium or central archive. And what central archives do exist are, by their very nature, not amenable to easy correlation. Two facts must commend themselves to the attention of a single individual to be combined; a billion facts are untenable for anyone.

Collection and connection are not separate and distinct activities. Often, what makes a fact memorable and worth passing on is its connection with other facts. Two facts, neither of which indicates anything alone, may in combination be quite indicative and for that reason merit further dissemination.

Detecting that a fact merits note and forwarding is, for its part, often composed of two factors: the awareness that something is a significant anomaly and the explanation of the anomaly as signifying something (e.g., is a terrorist precursor, is a new disease, is the sniper's car). We have analyzed seven compelling scenarios to learn about the barriers to recognition and forwarding. Four barriers stand out: lack of awareness, lack of attention, misuse of templates, and compartmentalization. Analysis of other vignettes may suggest other barriers, but these four seem to appear widely.

In the cases cited, finding the key facts appears to be the more difficult task; drawing conclusions from them is often easier (e.g., in the Belgrade bombing, the conclusions jump out immediately). We note four techniques for overcoming the barriers: networking, categorization, collaboration, and understanding roles and responsibilities. In the latter case, those roles and responsibilities can be viewed as three types:

- Perceivers, who recognize that something is notable;
- Decisionmakers, who decide on the degree of importance and on who should know about it; and
- Communicators, who make the fact known to those who should know of its existence.

Any solution using these roles and techniques to overcome the barriers must necessarily incorporate knowledge from many disciplines. The field of knowledge management tells us that knowledge can be of two types: explicit and tacit. Although it is easier to capture and tag explicit knowledge, it is the tacit knowledge that may prove to be more useful in making decisions about needs and knowns. We use psychology and sociology to help us understand context and hierarchy, without which we cannot evaluate the importance of each known or determine who should be aware of it. Technology can play a useful role, in sorting through large amounts of information, storing it, and communicating it within and across communities. But the technology must be supplemented with human intervention and interaction. Humans can recognize patterns more easily than machines; working together, humans and technology can identify anomalies and assess whether and why they are notable.

It is particularly important to recognize that tagging and organizing information is not enough. Information overload is a significant problem, and unless notable events make themselves known insistently and consistently, those who have a need to know about them will overlook them. At the same time, organizational structures (both for data and for people) can hinder as well as help in the recognition process. Underlings hesitate to interrupt superiors, and data stored in one category may not be recognized as belonging to other categories as well. It is for these reasons that new approaches are needed, based on lessons we must learn from the fuzzier sides of life that are less amenable to straightforward technological solutions.

In this document, we propose to define a set of institutional and technological processes that would enhance the ability to juxtapose scattered knowledge with other relevant scattered knowledge or needs more frequently and correctly (and without great harm to other operations) than we currently know how to do. Our approach brings together the social sciences and the information sciences in ways that leverage the best each has to offer. Having described the motivation for solving the problem and built a heuristic model of the problem space, we suggest an initial solution framework that involves five subprocesses: an In-Box Monitor to determine what we know, a Synthesizer to characterize it, an Analyzer to determine if it is important, a Decision Tool to decide who should know about it, and a Communicator to transmit it to those with need for it. From there, we sketch a research agenda to bring us closer to designing and implementing a solution. We note three steps toward achieving the goal of effective and efficient dot collection, including measures to help us understand and improve as we match needs with knowns.

References

Bieber, M., D. Engelbart, R. Furuta, S. R. Hiltz, J. Noll, J. Preece, E. A. Stohr, M. Turoff, and B. Van de Walle. 2000. "Toward Virtual Community Knowledge Evolution." *Journal of Management Information Systems* 18(4): 11–35.

Brown, John Seely, and Paul Duguid. 2000. *The Social Life of Information.* Boston, Mass.: Harvard Business School Press.

Burt, R. 1992. *Structural Holes: The Social Structure of Competition.* Cambridge, Mass.: Harvard University Press.

Burt, R. 1999. "Entrepreneurs, Distrust and Third Parties: A Strategic Look at the Dark Side of Dense Networks." In *Shared Cognition in Organizations*, ed. L. Thompson, J. Levine, and D. Messick. Mahweh, N.J.: Lawrence Erlbaum Associates.

Carley, Kathleen. 1986. "Knowledge Acquisition as a Social Phenomenon." *Instructional Science* 14(3–4): 381–438.

Carley, Kathleen. 1990. "Structural Constraints on Communication: The Diffusion of the Homomorphic Signal Analysis Technique through Scientific Fields." *Journal of Mathematical Sociology* 15(3–4): 207–246.

Carley, Kathleen M. 2002a. "Inhibiting Adaptation." In *Proceedings of the 2002 Command and Control Research and Technology Symposium*, Naval Postgraduate School, Monterey, Calif. Vienna, Va.: Evidence Based Research.

Carley, Kathleen M. 2002b. "Smart Agents and Organizations of the Future." In *The Handbook of New Media*, ed. Leah Lievrouw and Sonia Livingstone. Thousand Oaks, Calif.: Sage Publications, 206–220.

Carley, Kathleen M. 2003. "Dynamic Network Analysis." In *Summary of the NRC Workshop on Social Network Modeling and Analysis*, ed. Ron

Breiger and Kathleen M. Carley. Washington, D.C.: National Research Council.

Carley, Kathleen M., and Vanessa Hill. 2001. "Structural Change and Learning Within Organizations." In *Dynamics of Organizations: Computational Modeling and Organizational Theories*, ed. Alessandro Lomi and Erik R. Larsen. Cambridge, Mass.: MIT Press/AAAI Press/Live Oak, 63–92.

Carley, Kathleen M., Ju-Sung Lee, and David Krackhardt. 2001. "Destabilizing Networks." *Connections* 24(3): 31–34.

Carley, Kathleen M., and Yuqing Ren. 2001. "Tradeoffs Between Performance and Adaptability for C3I Architectures." In *Proceedings of the 2001 Command and Control Research and Technology Symposium*, Annapolis, Maryland, June 2001. Vienna, Va.: Evidence Based Research.

Carley, Kathleen M., and Craig Schreiber. 2002. "Information Technology and Knowledge Distribution in C3I Teams." In *Proceedings of the 2002 Command and Control Research and Technology Symposium Conference*, Naval Postgraduate School, Monterey, Calif. Vienna, Va.: Evidence Based Research.

Charniak, Eugene. 1994. *Statistical Language Learning*. Cambridge, Mass.: MIT Press.

Clayton, S., and P. Foster. 2000. "Real World Knowledge Sharing." *Knowledge Management* 4(2): 26–28.

Earl, M. 2001. "Knowledge Management Strategies: Toward a Taxonomy." *Journal of Management Information Systems* 18(1): 215–233.

Fagin, Jane, et al. 1995. *Reasoning About Knowledge*. Cambridge, Mass.: MIT Press.

Filho, Roberto F., Agma Santos, J. M. Traina, Caetano Traina, Jr., and Christos Faloutsos. 2001. "Similarity Search Without Tears: The OMNI Family of All-Purpose Access Methods." *Proceedings of ICSE 2001*: 623–630.

Hansen, M. T., N. Nohria, and T. Tierney. 1999. "What's Your Strategy for Managing Knowledge?" *Harvard Business Review* 77(2): 106–116.

Hickins, M. 1999. "Xerox Shares Its Knowledge." *Management Review* 88 (8): 40–45.

Hilderman, R. J., and H. J. Hamilton. 2001. *Knowledge Discovery and Measures of Interest*. Boston, Mass.: Kluwer Academic Press.

Hintikka, Jaakko. 1962. *Knowledge and Belief: An Introduction to the Logic of the Two Notions*. Ithaca, N.Y.: Cornell University Press.

Jacobs, Jane. 1961. *The Death and Life of Great American Cities*. New York: Random House.

Jelinek, Frederick. 1998. *Statistical Methods for Speech Recognition*. Cambridge, Mass.: MIT Press.

Jensen, Finn. 2001. *Bayesian Networks and Decision Graphs*. New York: Springer.

Kankanhalli, Atreyi, Fransiski Tanudidjaja, Juliana Sutanto, and Bernard C.Y. Tan. 2003. "The Role of IT in Successful Knowledge Management Initiatives." *Communications of the ACM* 46 (September): 69–73.

Kantardzic, Mehmed. 2003. *Data Mining: Concepts, Models, Methods and Algorithms*. New York: Wiley Interscience.

Klein, Gary. 1998. *Sources of Power: How People Make Decisions*. Cambridge, Mass.: MIT Press.

Kleiner, Art, and George Roth. 2000. "How to Make Experience Your Best Teacher." *Harvard Business Review on Knowledge Management*. Boston, Mass.: HBS Press, 172–177.

Langewische, William. 2002. *American Ground: The Unbuilding of the World Trade Center*. New York: HarperCollins Books.

Lee, Wenke, Salvatore J. Stolfo, Philip K. Chan, Eleazar Eskin, Wei Fan, Matthew Miller, Shlomo Hershkop and Junxin Zhang. 2001. "Real Time Data Mining-Based Intrusion Detection." *Proceedings of the Second DARPA Information Survivability Conference and Exposition*: 85–100.

Lesser, E. L., and J. Storck. 2001. "Communities of Practice and Organizational Performance." *IBM Systems Journal* 40(4): 831–841.

Manning, Christopher, and Hinrich Schutze. 1999. *Foundations of Statistical Natural Language Processing*. Cambridge, Mass.: MIT Press.

McDermott, Richard. 1999a. "How Information Technology Inspired, But Cannot Deliver Knowledge Management." *California Management Review* (41) 103–117.

McDermott, Richard. 1999b. "Learning Across Teams: The Role of Communities of Practice in Information Organizations." *Knowledge/Management Review* (May/June).

Mertins, K., P. Heisig, and J. Vorbeck. 2001. *Knowledge Management: Best Practices in Europe*. New York: Springer.

Nonaka, I., and H. Takeuchi. 1995. *The Knowledge Creating Company*. New York: Oxford University Press.

Papadimitriou, Spiros, Hiroyuki Kitagawa, Phillip B. Gibbons, and Christos Faloutsos. 2003. "LOCI: Fast Outlier Detection Using the Local Correlation Integral." *ICDE Proceedings 2003*, Bangalore.

Pearl, Judea. 2000. *Causality: Models, Reasoning, and Inference*. Cambridge, U.K.: Cambridge University Press.

Peters, Charles. 2002. "Tilting at Windmills." *Washington Monthly* (December): 5.

Pfleeger, Charles, and Shari Lawrence Pfleeger. 2003. *Security in Computing*. Third Edition, Saddle River, N.J.: Prentice Hall.

Preece, Jennifer. 2000. *Online Communities: Designing Usability, Supporting Sociability*. Chichester, U.K.: John Wiley and Sons.

Preece, Jennifer. 2003. "Tacit Knowledge and Social Capital: Supporting Sociability in Online Communities of Practice." *Proceedings of I-KNOW (Third International Conference on Knowledge Management) 2003*, Graz, Austria, ed. K. Tochtermann and H. Maurer, 72–78.

Prieto-Díaz, Rubén, and Peter Freeman. 1987. "Classifying Software for Reusability." *IEEE Software* 4 (January): 6–17.

Putnam, Robert. 2000. *Bowling Alone: The Collapse and Revival of American Community*. New York: Simon and Schuster.

Rasmussen, Jens. 1986. *Information Processing and Human-Machine Interaction: An Approach to Cognitive Engineering*. New York: North Holland.

Shannon, Claude E. 1948. "A Mathematical Theory of Communication." *Bell System Technical Journal* 27 (July and October): 379-423, 623-56.

Spirtes, Peter, et al. 2000. *Causation, Prediction and Search*. 2nd ed. Cambridge, Mass.: MIT Press.

Strasser, Gerland, and Beth Dietz-Uhler. 2001. "Collective Choice, Judgment, and Problem-Solving." In *Blackwell Handbook of Social Psychology: Group Processes*, ed. Michael A. Hogg and R. Scott Tindale. Oxford, U.K.: Blackwell Publishers, 31–55.

Thuraisingham, Bhavani. 2001. *Managing and Mining Multimedia Databases*. Boca Raton, Fla.: CRC Press.

Traina, Caetano, Agma Juci, Machado Traina, Leejay Wu, and Christos Faloutsos. 2000. "Fast Feature Selection Using the Fractal Dimension." *XV Brazilian Symposium on Databases (SBBD)*, Joao Pessoa, Brazil.

U.S. House of Representatives. 2003. "Politics and Science in the Bush Administration," Committee on Government Reform, Minority Report, August. Available at www.reform.house.gov/min.

Wang, Mengzhi, Tara Madhyastha, Ngai Hang Chan, Spiros Papadimitriou, and Christos Faloutsos 2002. "Data Mining Meets Performance Evaluation: Fast Algorithms for Modeling Bursty Traffic." *ICDE Proceedings 2002*, San Jose, California.

Watts, Duncan. 1999. *Small Worlds: The Dynamics of Networks between Order and Randomness*. Princeton, N.J.: Princeton University Press.

Watts, Duncan, and Steven Strogatz. 1998. "Collective Dynamics of 'Small-World' Networks." *Nature* 393 (4 June): 440–442.

Wenger, Etienne. 1996. "How to Optimize Organizational Learning." *Healthcare Forum Journal* (July/August), 22–23.

Wenger, Etienne. 1998. *Communities of Practice: Learning, Meaning and Identity*. Cambridge, U.K.: Cambridge University Press.

Wenger, Etienne, Richard McDermott, and William M. Snyder. 2002. *Cultivating Communities of Practice*. Cambridge, Mass.: Harvard Business School Press.

Wohlstetter, Roberta. 1962. *Pearl Harbor: Warning and Decision*. Stanford, Calif.: Stanford University Press.

Wu, Leejay, and Christos Faloutsos. 2002. "Making Every Bit Count: Fast Nonlinear Axis Scaling." *Proceedings of the Eighth ACM SIGKDD International Conference on Knowledge Discovery and Data Mining*.